They Were Family:

Pre-Stonewall History & Photographs of the LGBTQIA+ Community

By Mason Kaye

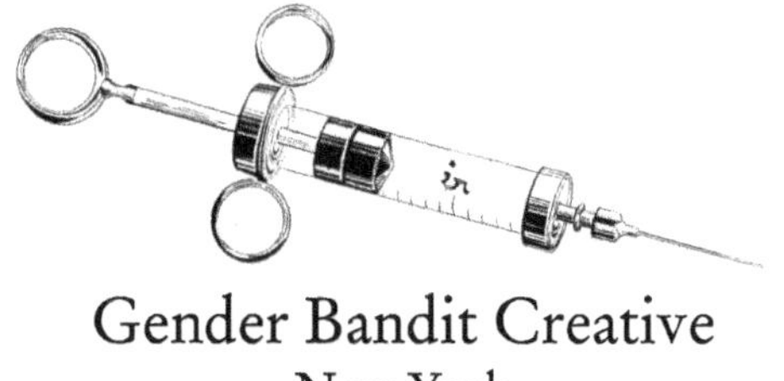

Gender Bandit Creative
New York

ISBN 978-0-578-32638-2

Gender Bandit Creative
101 Greenwich St. Fl. 2
New York, NY 10006
www.genderbanditcreative.com

To the family (blood, chosen, and fur alike) that supported this dream.
Particularly to these three,
Katherine, Jaimie and Bader

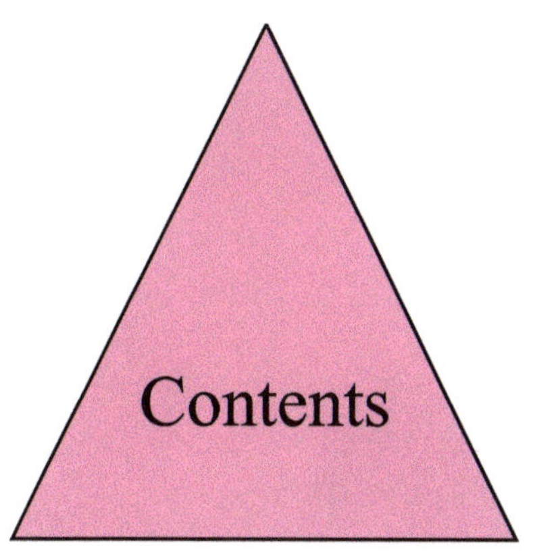
Contents

Introduction: Welcome to the Family

In its most basic definition, *They Were Family* is a historic photo and fact book. Specifically, it is a brief overview of pre-Stonewall LGBTQIA+ history told through facts, photographs, and genuine queer sass. It is the culmination of almost a decade of specific research and collecting original photos, combined with a lifetime passion for all things human history. I named it for the common LGBTQIA+ phrase "they're family," which is used to covertly reference another queer person in conversation, and finds origins in the secret gay language, Polari (which you will learn about in this book). It all started because in my reading of history something that I rarely saw was my own identity reflected back at me. The queer history I was taught rarely dated further back than 1969, as if LGBTQIA+ and gender diverse people just sprouted into existence at the Stonewall Riots. I wanted so badly to see myself in history, to see the successes of other queer individuals, and to know where I came from so I can truly appreciate where I am and fight for where I need to go. Representation matters, and that absolutely includes education and history.

So, I began to do my own research and soon realized something that many marginalized groups experience; clearly, it was not that LGBTQIA+ people just weren't around, it's that for centuries our history and stories have either been rewritten, hidden, or destroyed, and I mean that quite literally. From loving queer relationships being referred to in textbooks as "close friendships," to the burning of queer research by the Nazis in WWII, all the way down to families eliminating any trace of notes or photos of queer relatives, our history was deliberately pushed into obscurity, but it was not eliminated completely.

I started to find an abundance of "family" throughout human existence, so keep in mind that *They Were Family* truly just scratches the surface of Queer history. I could have written ten more books, and entire books on each of the facts they contained, and if there is something that sparks your interest then research it more! Some of the names here are famous, others are more obscure people, but all of it is our history, and not just LGBTQIA+ people, but all of us as humans.

When I was creating this book, besides wanting it to be easily digestible, I wanted it to be personal. So, I included photographs from my own collection, to give faces to the often-forgotten queer lives of the past. The collection started with a single photo from an antique store that showed a very obviously lesbian couple. The joy I felt at seeing a tintype, a 150-year-old piece of tangible proof, of the LGBTQIA+ community, is indescribable. My collection grew, and so, in this book there are more than one hundred photos of the "everyday" LGBTQIA+ person, including gay men, lesbians, drag queens, transgender men and women, and everyone in between and outside. (These photographs are not directly related to the facts, unless noted.)

They Were Family is meant to be a small, yet vital, window into a past that is so often overlooked. It is meant to tell some of the stories of the legendary people who came before us. Most importantly, it is meant to provide some kid who feels like me a chance to see themselves in history and know that they don't have to try to fit in because we were always meant to stand out.

Important Notes:

First, on my inclusion of Indigenous cultures and people in this book. It needs to be clear that in no way can Indigenous identities (both in historical context and in current times) be summed up as "gay" or "trans." Their identities are deeply tied to their cultures, and thus, deserve respect as their own separate entities. The reason I have included facts about Indigenous people is simple, in that their mere existence millennia ago is proof that the gender binary and heteronormativity are social constructs, and rather new ones at that.

Second, I will be referring to humans in this book using the pronouns they used for themselves or based on the way they presented in their lives (this includes the use of non-binary pronouns, they/them, even though those are not used in in historical texts). As well, the only reason certain people's birth names are included is for research and historical context. Many of these people had names they went by, but throughout history that was negated or erased, so in order to do further education, their birth names must be included. The reason I note this here is because the name someone uses is their name. At no point is someone's birth name important, needed, or your business, in everyday life.

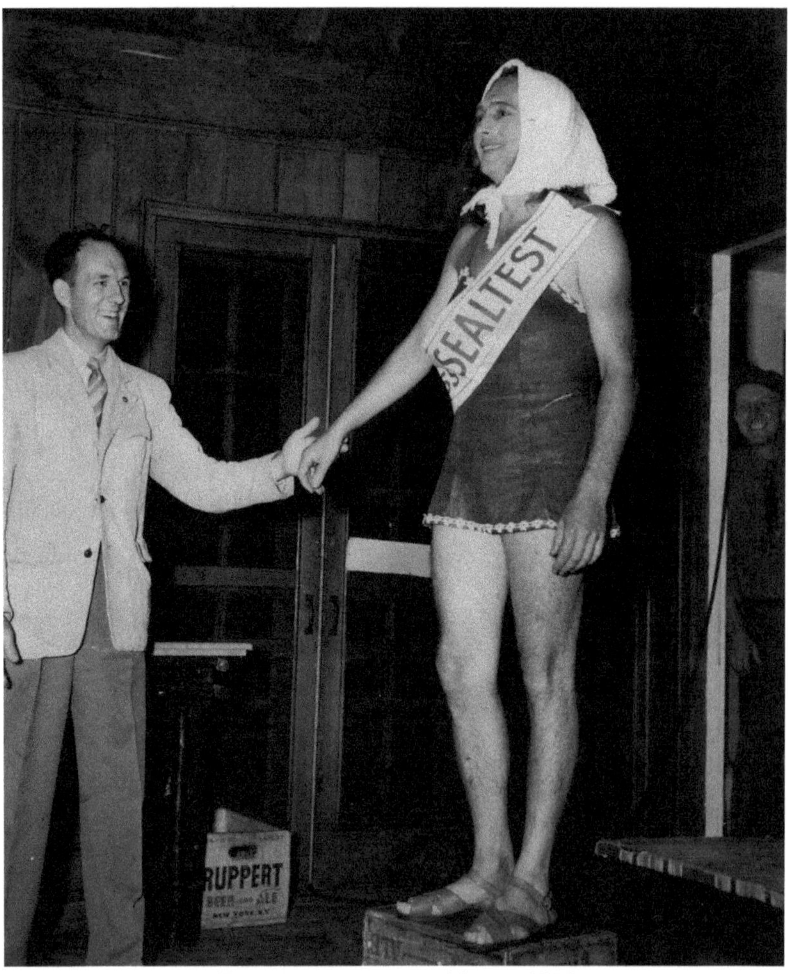

Drag queen competition c.1920

Chapter One: We Were Carved in Stone (10,000 BCE - 1599 CE)

Around 12,000 years ago humans started making erotic cave art, from stone carvings to wall paintings, and when they did, queer sex was included. It was not a fluke of Stone Age inclusion either, and I do mean Stone Age, with a bit of the Bronze Age thrown in (the art described below dates from 10,000-1 BCE). In Sicily, on the wall of a cave there is an image of a group of men in bird masks surrounding a gay couple, also in bird masks, doing what the "birds and the bees" do. The crudely scratched picture is perfectly clear and was discovered when part of the site was exposed after a bombing during WWII. A scene of same-sex love is depicted in Norway, showing two male-bodied figures locked together, with numerous others around them also engaged in various sex acts. Sweden is home to a quite a few cave art pieces that are considered to represent wedding ceremonies, and in several of these the bride-like figure is drawn with a penis, which could indicate the presence of gender variation beyond the binary or show Stone Age marriage for the gay community. In Zimbabwe, though erotic cave art is rare in general, there are still queer images found, mainly attributed to the San people and dating from around 1 BCE. Spain is where the largest number of intimate queer situations are shown, with a wide range of differing sex acts. Some of these drawings are considered to be the most detailed of any prehistoric cave art. The list could go on and on, and these are just the cave drawings that have survived and that we have discovered.

Queer sex was included when early humans created erotic art, and so gender-diverse people were included when they spoke about or showed images of the human body. Dating back to somewhere between 7,000-1,000 BCE, some carved stone figurines found in the Mediterranean depict bodies with breasts and a penis; others show no sex characteristics at all. They are very similar to the Venus figurines commonly seen in prehistoric art, "Venus" being the name given to the figures carved to depict the naked form of a body assigned female at birth, usually in a rounded shape. Then there are the pottery sherds dating to the Middle Kingdom of Egypt (2,000-1,800 BCE), that list recognized genders of the empire. For Egyptians, there was something beyond a simple binary, most likely due to the fact that the binary was not invented for another 3,500 years or so. The list of genders that were shown on the pottery were: tai (male), hmt (female), and a third gender, sḫt ("sekhet").

A step further in LGBTQIA+ prehistoric existence comes from Prague, where a burial site dating from about 2800 to 2500 BCE was discovered to hold a body that would have been assigned male at birth, but with female-associated funeral rites completed. Typically, males were buried facing west, and this human was facing east. Males were also buried with knives and hammers; this human had pots and jugs, associated with female burials. Shamans of the time were buried in the female manner, but their burial sites are extravagant, with jewelry and detailed art, while this site lacked anything like that. The site for our queer ancestor was quite simply that of an everyday female of the period. The gender she was assigned at birth clearly had no bearing on how society viewed her, even in death.

❧ ❧ ❧ ❧

It was not only the pharaohs of Egypt who had the honor of being placed in a tomb, and in 1964, in the necropolis at Saqqara, Egypt, the tomb of Khnumhotep and Niankhkhnum was discovered dating back to 2400 BCE. A tomb for two people was not unusual—married couples were often buried together—but what stood out about this one was that these two people were both assigned male at birth. The two held relatively high status and shared the title of Overseer of the Manicurists in the Palace of King Nyuserre Ini, sixth pharaoh of the Fifth Dynasty. Their tomb was adorned with images that displayed the men in intimate positions, like those of husband-and-wife tombs. In traditional burial images the husband and wife are pictured facing each other, and in this tomb

Khnumhotep and Niankhkhnum are depicted in this way. It was not a single room either; the inner hall, the outer hall, the forecourt, the inner vestibule, the outer vestibule, every inch of this tomb holds countless displays of Khnumhotep and Niankhkhnum sitting as loving life partners, including the epigraph that reads, “Joined in life and joined in death.”

❧ ❧ ❧ ❧

Mesopotamia is considered the birthplace of civilization, and since LGBTQIA+ people have existed forever and the gender binary has not, it should be no shock that in Mesopotamian mythology there is reference to gender variation. A Sumerian creation myth found carved into a stone tablet from 2000 BCE tells the story of the mother goddess of the mountains, Ninḫursaĝ, and the goddess of creation, Namma, creating mankind out of clay. As they created the different bodies of humans, they came to make a third gender category that had no sex characteristics and was meant to be special. When giving “class” and status to the sets of humans, this third variant of human was said to “stand before the king” , noting a unique place in society. In this story, as was common, the gender diverse group outside of the modern-day binary is viewed as something that should be held in high regard or is intrinsically extraordinary.

❧ ❧ ❧ ❧

The Binary is Basic

Though people have lived outside the gender binary since the beginning of human history, most people find tracking LGBTQIA+ narratives difficult. One of the reasons is that we try to find our past by looking for words like “gay,” “lesbian,” or “transgender” or for people to match these definitions exactly, but the fact is these Western terms have come into our language only in the last two centuries, and they certainly do not encompass the vast history that occurred before and after they were coined. This list is simply the tip of the iceberg of gender variations that have existed and continue to exist in our world today. Some of these identities date back to at least 1000 BCE and are seen in more than 150 Indigenous tribes in North America alone (the term “two-spirit” is an umbrella term created in 1990 that refers to the many gender variations that exist among these groups of people). Many of these terms are deeply tied to the culture of which they are a part, and so we cannot just boil them down to simply being “transgender” people.

*A note to always remember: Gender identity and sexuality are two different concepts, and do not have mutually exclusive pairings.

Akava'ine and ‘Akatāne - Cook Islands, Māori - More modern terms, both words come from the prefix *aka* meaning “to behave like.” With the latter half of each meaning *va'ine* “woman” and *tāne* “man," these terms are pretty direct in giving separate status to humans who fall outside the binary. As with most Indigenous populations, Pacific Island communities have historically held cultural places for gender-diverse people but with the arrival of European colonizers in the nineteenth century came a sharp decline in the acceptance of these humans.

A'yai-kik-ahsi and Ninauh-oskitsi-pahpyaki - North America, Blackfeet Nation - Meaning “acts like a woman," A'yai-kik-ahsi refers to people assigned male at birth who express their gender in a feminine manner and were revered as spiritual leaders and warriors. Ninauh-oskitsi-pahpyaki means “manly hearted woman” and refers to people assigned female at birth who presented masculine in their clothing and aesthetics and were feared warriors in combat.

Baklâ (Bayot in Binisaya, Agî in Ilonggo) and Tomboy (Binalaki in Tagalog) - Philippines - Baklâ is a term whose meaning has evolved over time, for a group of people who have always existed. Baklâ now refers to people assigned male at birth who express their gender in a feminine way. In pre-colonial times, many baklâ people were highly regarded as spiritual leaders. Tomboy, similarly, refers to someone assigned female at birth who expresses their gender in a masculine way. Though known by many labels, people who fall under the title of baklâ or tomboy are a standard part of Filipino culture.

Bissu, Calalai, and Calabai - Indonesia, Burgis People - These three gender variations come from the Burgis people who observe a gender spectrum that contains five separate genders and derives from ancient religious rituals. Calalai refers to people who were assigned female at birth, and present in a masculine form, interacting in society in a culturally male way; while calabai refers to people who were assigned male and present in a feminine way. (There is a specific group of people who fall into the calabai category in Indonesia called "**waria**," who are people who have a "woman's soul in a man's body.") Bissu people are considered to be androgynous, or "gender transcendent," and through the 1940s were a central part of rituals in society.

Faʻafafine - Samoa - A recognized gender in both Samoan and American Samoan culture, fa'afafine people are assigned male at birth and embody traditionally Samoan male and female gender expressions. They personify the tradition of tautau, or service to family, that is core to the community, usually taking part in the matriarchal categorized roles. This role of caregiver is commonly seen amongst gender-diverse people.

Fakaleitī - Tonga - Similar to fa'afafine people, the term fakaleitī refers to people who are assigned male at birth and express their gender in a feminine way. The literal translation being "like a lady." In Nukuʻalofa, the capital of Tonga, the annual Miss Galaxy Pageant is held, which is a beauty competition exclusively for fakaleitī people.

Femminielli (Femminiello -singular) - Naples - Seen as a sign of luck in Neapolitan culture, femminielli people are assigned male at birth and present in a feminine way. There are still smaller traditions that involve femminielli, like the Wedding of Zeza, which is celebrated every year in the town of Pagani, Italy. It is not actually a celebration of a wedding, but the acting out of a scene from the sixteenth century's Commedia dell'arte.

Hemaneh - North America, Cheyenne Nation - A literal translation of "half man, half woman," hemaneh people are assigned male at birth and present in a feminine manner. Hemaneh people were at one time shamans renowned for their healing abilities, the last two shamans passing away in 1879.

Hijra - India - Known as khawaja sira in Pakistan, and sometimes referred to as Kinnar, a mythical being in the Hindu culture (spelled Kinnara), hijra people are a recognized third gender in India, and have been specifically documented for at least 400 years. The existence of a tritiya prakriti ("third nature") in India as a general concept, however, dates to at least 400 BCE. This idea of a third gender is referenced in the *Kama Sutra*, and the *Rāmāyana* (which is one of the oldest Sanskrit epics).

Ininiikaaz and Ikwekaazo - North America, Ojibwe People - These terms translate as “one who endeavors to be like a man” and “one who endeavors to be like a woman," respectively.

Koekchuch - Russia, Itelmens of Siberia - This gender variant no longer exists, due to the Itelmen culture slowly being lost over time (only one in five people speak the native language, with most now speaking Russian). Koekchuch people were common at least through the eighteenth century, when the Russian explorer Stepan Krasheninnikov observed their place in society.

Lhamana - North America, Zuni People - In 1886, when a Zuni delegation went to Washington DC to meet President Cleveland (who was both the 22nd and 24th president), gender diverse people were represented in the body of We’wha, a lhamana-identifying person (more on them later). Lhamana people are assigned male at birth and present typically in a feminine way; but unlike some other gender variants where gender presentation then denotes societal role, lhamana people will often perform tasks that are considered male as well as some that are considered female.

Māhū - Hawai’i - A term dating back well before colonial Hawai’i, this to-the-point term means “in the middle.” For māhū people, what you are assigned at birth does not matter, and they embody male- and female-associated gender traits. They were regarded as healers and teachers, particularly of the hula; even now they are responsible for passing down traditions and lessons on balance and connection. In the modern usage, there are up to five designations of māhū people: emotionally, spiritually, psychologically and culturally feeling- ha'akāne (male), ha'awahine (female) and physically presenting - ho'okāne (male), ho'owahine (female), and the traditional māhū.

Mudoko Dako - Uganda, Lango People - This is a gender identity that was prevalent in pre-colonial Africa among not only Lango people, but the Karamojan and Teso people as well. Mudoko Dako people were not assigned female at birth, but socially and culturally took on the traditional role of female-presenting people in society.

Mukhannathun (Mukhannath- singular) - Saudi Arabia - Meaning "feminine ones" or "ones who resemble women," this gender variant dates to at least the year 600. In classical Arabic texts, they were associated with music and entertainment and were thriving members of society.

Muxe - Mexico, Zapotec Culture - A standard third gender in Oaxaca, Mexico, there are typically two variations of muxe people that are recognized: vestidas ("dressed," i.e., wearing clothing typically associated with female-presenting people) and pintadas ("painted," i.e., wearing makeup with clothing typically associated with male-presenting people). Muxe people are known to maintain traditional Zapotec dress, language, and other cultural customs of the region.

Nádleehi - North America, Diné (Navajo) Nation - A variant that is based around the Navajo gender spectrum, which holds at least four variations of gender, nádleehi people can potentially present differently day-to-day, and will typically hold female associated roles in society.

Quariwarmi - Peru, Inca Civilization - A gender variation that originated in pre-colonial Peru, and still exists today, meaning "man-woman," many quariwarmi people were and are shamans, or spiritual leaders, with close ties to Chuquichinchay, a golden jaguar deity.

Sekrata - Madagascar, Antandroy and Hova People - Believed to be highly spiritual and sacred, sekrata people are part of the social landscape of some tribes in Madagascar. Assigned male at birth, sekrata people express their gender in a feminine way. They are also considered some of the most talented dancers and entertainers.

Ubhatovyañjanaka - Sri Lanka - A term dating back at least to the founding of Buddhism around 400 BCE, ubhatovyañjanaka refers to people who present with male and female characteristics, sometimes interpreted as intersex people. Two other gender variants observed in Sri Lanka are **vepurisikā** people, who are assigned male at birth and present in a feminine way, and **sambhinna**, which refers to "sexual indistinctness" or androgynous people.

Winyanktehca - Lakota Nation - This old Lakota gender variant translates as "to be like a woman." Winyanktehca people were a recognized social class who operated in what would be considered the female spectrum of Lakota society. One of Sitting Bull's (1831-1890) five wives was a winyanktehca person. "Winkte," which derives from Winyanktehca, is used in modern times to refer to gay men.

Sapphic and **lesbian** are both words for which we must thank the lyric poet, Sappho (c.630- c.570 BCE). Born on the island of Lesbos, Sappho was a prolific writer, who was famous enough in her own time to have her works "published" by Athenian merchants and Alexandrian scholars (yes, thousands of lines of poetry were handwritten so they could be shared; her work was that good). Though only fragmented lines of her works remains, her overtly lesbian prose have garnered her lasting fame, to the point that female-presenting love is named after both her and her home island. In a hilariously wasteful 2008 court case, three residents of Lesbos actually attempted to sue to stop the word "lesbian" from being used for/by gay women. They lost.

One of the original symbols of the republic in ancient Greece were the lovers Harmodius and Aristogeiton; and that is because in 514 BCE they committed tyrannicide (killing of an unjust ruler or tyrant) and set in motion a chain of events that brought democracy to Athens. Their original plot did not go according to plan, and in the chaos, they were only able to kill one of their targets and they, themselves, were killed and arrested, respectively, but that was enough success. With their actions a heavy enough blow to tyranny was struck, and within six years reforms from Cleisthenes were put in place that laid the groundwork for democracy. Harmodius and Aristogeiton's sacrifices did not go unnoticed: statues were erected for them, some of the first non-god statues in ancient Greece.

❧ ❧ ❧ ❧

The foundation of much of modern Western thought, from politics to medicine, is credited to the minds of ancient Greece and Rome. One of those thinkers was Hippocrates (c.460- c.370 BCE), the namesake of the physicians' *Hippocratic Oath*, and he viewed gender beyond a binary. In his work, Hippocrates documented multiple intersex patients and their naturally occurring state in the world. "Intersex" is a word that applies to humans who are born with internal and/or external sex characteristics that are not necessarily exclusive to those assigned as male or female. Statistically, intersex people make up, at a minimum of, 1.7% of the world population (conservative estimate), or approximately

132,600,000 people. Another way to frame it is: imagine 40% of the US population born existing outside of the binary (the term "intersex" was coined by geneticist Richard Goldschmidt in 1915). Greek historian Diodorus Siculus (c.90- c.30 BCE), remarked that intersex children were regarded as prodigies and oracles of sorts. Pliny the Elder (c.23-79 CE), a Roman philosopher, noted intersex people in his encyclopedic work, *Naturalis Historia* (Natural History), "those who are born of both sexes, whom we call... at one time androgyni." Some etymology on the word "androgynous": it derives from the Greek "andr-" meaning man, and "gyn" meaning woman.

❧ ❧ ☙ ☙

The *Kama Sutra* is one of the most well-known erotic texts of all time. An often-overlooked aspect of this work in the Western world, however, is that it is much more than just a book on various sex positions. Written in India, somewhere around 400-200 BCE, the *Kama Sutra* is a book about living well, maintaining love, and fulfilling all of life's pleasures with that ecstasy not confined by a binary narrative. Multiple chapters detail pleasure and love across the gender spectrum and include reference to tritiya prakriti, or "third nature." Though the concept of the third nature has been interpreted variously over time, from queer men to a gender variant like hijra people, what it has come to represent is the natural existence of people that live outside of cis/heteronormativity.

❧ ❧ ☙ ☙

Just like modern teens writing their significant other's initials on a wall or making a wish on an eyelash for forever love, the queer lovers of the past did the same in their own way. On the island of Astypalaia in Greece, stone carvings from circa 500-300 BCE were discovered that essentially marked the location where a gay couple had sex. Next to numerous carved phallic symbols, a rather bold inscription translates to, "Nikasitimos (Νικασίτιμος) was here mounting Timion (Τιμίονα)." Another piece of affection left over from history is a lead tablet from around 400 BCE that was carved with a binding or love spell. This spell was commissioned by Sophia to have Gorgonia become attracted and tied to her for life. Part of the spell reads, "Burn, Burn. Set on fire, inflame. Inflame her soul, heart, liver, spirit with love."

❧ ❧ ❧ ❧

Around 385 BCE the world was given Plato's (c.428- c.348 BCE) *Symposium*, a dialogue, so-to-speak, of praise for the god of love, Eros, by some of ancient Greece's most notable thinkers. One of the speeches given in the work is by Aristophanes (c.446- c.386 BCE), and tells a version of the creation myth, one that is commonly referred to as "the origin of love," (If you have seen *Hedwig & the Angry Inch* this might seem familiar). The story goes that humans originally came in three forms: males, who descended from the Sun, and were two male-assigned bodies attached, females, who descended from the Earth, and were two female-assigned bodies attached, and then androgynous, who descended from the Moon, and were a female-assigned body and male-assigned body attached. Humans became too powerful, and Zeus was not a fan of this, but did not want to smite humans completely because they gave the gods sacrifices, so instead, he sliced us all in half, having Apollo heal the wounds by pulling our skin to form a tiny reminder on our belly, the navel. Zeus' plan was to have the core of our power, our connection to each other, removed so that we were no longer a threat and would spend our time searching for our other half.

Something to note, current understanding of heterosexual couples are that of the Moon, and are considered the androgynous, or third nature in this scenario.

☙ ☙ ❧ ❧

If there is any proof in the power of connection that Zeus was threatened by in the origin of love myth, it is that of the Sacred Band of Thebes, who remained undefeated in battle from 378-338 BCE. This small, but incredibly mighty army was made up of 300 men, or more accurately, 150 gay couples. The idea for this type of "gay army" came from the notion that there is nothing a person will fight harder for than their love, and that was certainly proven true with the Sacred Band's track record. Their fame began with their major victory over another famous 300, the Spartans in 371 BCE, and they continued on this path for more than thirty years. Their triumphs finally came to an end in 338 BCE, when they fought until every one of their lives was lost against another ancient queer legend, Alexander the Great, at the Battle of Chaeronea. As a full circle moment, Alexander's father, Phillip II (c.382-336 BCE), like his son, was known to have gay relationships and was actually a student of General Epaminondas (c.418-362 BCE), one of the heads of the Sacred Band of Thebes.

☙ ☙ ❧ ❧

There are many euphemisms that exist for queer relationships and love, and most come from some historical reference. One of those that is quite popular in Asia and has a rather beautiful origin story, is "cut sleeve" or "breaking the sleeve." The story behind this comes from the Han Dynasty in China, which is known for numerous queer emperors, beginning with the first, Emperor Gaozu (256-195 BCE) and his favorite lover, Ji Ru. The "cut sleeve" comes from the life of another Han ruler, Emperor Ai (27 BCE - 1 CE) and the love he had for Dong Xian (23 BCE- 1 CE). Though Emperor Ai showered Dong Xian with titles and homes, even trying to leave the throne to him, it was a more innocent act that led to this saying. One day they were both taking a nap, the emperor holding Dong Xian, when he needed to get up to go to a meeting. Instead of waking his sleeping partner, Emperor Ai cut off the sleeve of his robe, leaving his partner unmoved, and proceeded to attend court with only one sleeve (fashion icon). The emperor's sweet move went on to inspire not only the gay community, but books and plays alike.

In the year 8, Ovid's crowning achievement *Metamorphoses* was published. This almost 12,000-line, 15-book work covers over 250 myths and centers around one core theme, in Ovid's own words, "I intend to speak of forms changed into new entities." The stories' subjects range from well-known names like Julius Caesar and Hercules, to lesser known, like Iphis. The tale of Iphis, from book IX, begins with his parents desiring to have a son, because they could not afford the dowry that a daughter would require. Iphis was assigned female at birth, but his mother hid this from everyone, including her husband, and raised Iphis as male. As he grew up, everything was basically working out, and he even fell in love with the girl next door, Ianthe. He prayed to the gods to have his sex assigned male, since his sex characteristics would determine his fate, and even his mother helped, bringing him to the temple of Isis. Isis came through granting him a gender-affirming miracle, and he and Ianthe were married, living happily ever after, with Hymenaios, the god of marriage, watching out for them always.

The volcanic eruption of Mount Vesuvius in the year 79 is one of the most famous moments in history, and one of the reasons for this is that the power of this eruption was so massive it literally engulfed entire villages, encapsulating them in ash and froze that moment in time. One of the things that came from the discovery of these time-capsule towns, was an enormous amount of erotic art. The way Pompeii and Herculaneum viewed the naked human body and sex across the gender spectrum was far more inclusive and open than in the 1700s, when they were uncovered (and today, quite honestly). There were hundreds of images, and many included queer bodies and sex acts. When King Francis I of Naples (1777-1830) went with his family to see an exhibit of the art in 1819, he was said to be "so embarrassed" by it that he had it hidden away as a Gabinetto Segreto (Secret Cabinet), a secret museum that cannot be viewed by the public. Over the last 200 years, the works have lived this cycle of being banned and then allowed for view again, currently being held at Naples' National Archaeological Museum.

❧ ❧ ❧ ❧

The emperors of ancient Rome were known for living lavish, out-of-the-ordinary lives, the tales of which could put even the best soap operas to shame. From the rise of Nero (37-68 CE) and his Domus Aurea to Hadrian (76-138) not only naming a wall for himself, but also entire cities after his lover Antinous who had drowned, the stories that remain are grandiose and often overtly queer. There is even one emperor of Rome who was perhaps the first transgender individual to rule in the Western world; her name was Elagabalus (c. 204-222). Though many emperors had relationships with or even married men, it was important never to be viewed as the "passive" or "submissive" partner in the situation within Ancient Rome and Greek culture, but for Elagabalus it was different. She was never supposed to be emperor, but after her grandmother deposed the previous ruler, Elagabalus was tapped at fourteen to head the Roman Empire. Roman statesman and historian Cassius Dio (c.155- c.235) wrote that Elagabalus preferred to be called Lady, Mistress, or even Queen of Hierocles (who was one of her favorite lovers), wore wigs and make-up, and had offered vast sums of money to any physician that could perform gender-affirming surgery for her (and with all of that, Elagabalus is still referred to using he/him pronouns). It was also widely known, in her short four-year rule, that Elagabalus was a sex worker, and a proud one at that. After growing tired of working in the taverns and brothels in Rome, she had a room built in her palace, which was specifically for "in-call," and was said to brag about her number of lovers and how much people would pay for her time.

❧ ❧ ❧ ❧

Loosely translated to "a special friend" and describing the bond between two women, motsoalle relationships in Basotho culture

(indigenous people of Lesotho, Africa) date back at least to the year 400. As with most culturally rooted concepts, motsoalle relationships are not simply the Western idea of lesbianism. They are bonds formed, usually as young teens, that were once celebrated and recognized in society, traditionally with a ceremony, like a wedding. They can cover a spectrum of relationship forms, from sexual partner to confidante, but always they are about true, meaningful connections that are more intimate than that of "straight" girl friends we see in modern, Western culture.

☙ ☙ ❧ ❧

Humans have a need to understand everything that is happening around us, and if there is not an available reason, we will create one. For instance, when the ancient Greeks did not know why thunder occurred, they created Zeus and blamed his anger, or when there were earthquakes and plagues in Constantinople in 534, queer people were blamed. This concept of finding a scapegoat for disasters or natural events is common, even seen with the Covid-19 outbreak. For the Byzantine Emperor Justinian I (482-565), who ruled during the first bubonic plague outbreak, he wrote in his Novella 141 about how he "predicted" the year before that gay people would be the cause of plagues, earthquakes, and pestilences. Again in 1519, a friar in Spain preached that the plague was "God's wrath for sodomy," which so enraged the poor, illness-stricken crowd that they then went and effectively hunted down gay men to burn at the stake. The obvious flaw in this logic, besides the belief that gay people control fate and the weather, is the existence of queer people outside of these periods of plagues; at no point are we cheered for making April 25 the perfect date, not too warm, not too cold, all you need is a light jacket.

❧ ❧ ❧ ❧

The love of men, women, and wine; what more could you want from a poem? Truly not much, and that is exactly what the classical Arabic poet, Abū Nuwās (c.755- c.813), composed. Though he was

not the originator of Arabic homoerotic poetry (his mentor and suspected lover, Wāliba ibn Hubāb, was also a writer of the genre), Nuwās is credited with effectively breaking the genre into the "mainstream" of both his own time and today. When his love poems were first distributed in the eighth century, they were done so in two main chapters: female-presenting love (muʾannathāt) and male-presenting love (mudhakkarāt), with several poems having an ambiguous love interest. His other great love was wine, and so on top of homoerotic poetry, he is also considered a pioneer of khamriyyāt or wine-poems. These poems all centered around wine, drinking wine, loving wine, and loving people who also love wine. Based on these topics, it is no wonder that Nuwās is one of the most translated Arabic poets of all time.

Basil I, the Macedonian (c.811-886) might be the original rags-to-riches story, going from living on the streets to Byzantine Emperor, all thanks to his charm, bisexuality, seduction, and some murder. Much of Basil I's early life is a mystery; what is known is that his family was enslaved in Bulgaria and when he was finally freed, he travelled from city to city, most likely making his way as a sex worker. In his early twenties he reached Constantinople and after falling asleep in a church doorway, his life would be changed. Basil I met an abbot at the church named Nicholas and they formed a relationship, one that was made official in a church ceremony (more on these marriages in a bit) that Nicholas officiated. The pair stayed together for years, but this was simply the first relationship of the soon-to-be emperor. Nicholas introduced Basil I to a member of the royal family, Theophilitzes, who became infatuated with him and hired him to work at the palace stables. From here Basil I met Danielis and her son, who became his next church-official relationship. Danielis not only approved of her son's relationship but became a mother figure for Basil I, even providing him with land and money, which set him up to be an equal among the social elite for whom he had been working. Basil I took this a step further and entered Emperor Michael III's (c.840-867) wrestling tournament, where he not only won the trophy, but also won the emperor's heart. He became Michael III's favorite partner, so much so that Basil I was made co-emperor on Michael III's request. This arrangement worked for a while, until Michael III's eyes fell on another man, and Basil I's future was threatened. So, he did what any vying emperor in the 800s would, and he assassinated his lover and became head ruler. During his 19-year reign, Basil I was well liked among his compatriots, particularly in comparison to his predecessor, and was able to help further establish the Byzantine empire as a power in the Mediterranean.

❧ ❧ ☙ ☙

Originally published in Damascus around the tenth century, *Jawami` al-ladhdha* (translating to the Delicious Pleasures,

Lesbian wedding ceremony (above) and party (below) real photo postcards, circa 1905.
(note: besides the heart decorations, the windows and doors are completely covered to maintain safety)

commonly known as *Encyclopedia of Pleasure*) is one of the oldest Arabic erotic books written, that still exists. Similar to Plato's *Symposium* in that numerous poets and authors tell stories, the *Encyclopedia of Pleasure* tells several tales of sex, love, pleasure, and the human body. One of the love stories is of al-Zarqā, an Arab woman who was a lesbian, and her lover al-Hurqah, a Christian woman. It tells of how strong their love for each other was, beyond anything else, to the point that when al-Zarqā passed away, al-Hurqah cut her hair, wore black, and swore to be alone until she herself died. Over the thousand years since *Encyclopedia of Pleasure* was published, the queer parts have been removed and then returned countless times, still being banned in numerous countries today.

❧ ❧ ❧ ❧

On April 16, 1061, Pedro Diaz and Muño Vandilaz were married by a priest in the Monastery of San Salvador de Celanova, in the Galicia region of Spain. Historically, it was not uncommon for LGBTQIA+ people to be married, even having a ceremony within the church. When it comes to gay men, in Christianity specifically, the ritual was referred to as adelphopoiesis or "brother-making." Some historians like to argue that this is just two really close friends, which for some might have been true (just like with straight marriages), but in the case of Diaz and Vandilaz, they, in front of witnesses, in a church, with a priest, vowed and signed legal documents to care for each other, share their assets and bed, work as partners and, “if Pedro dies before Muño, he will leave the property and documents to Muño. And if Muño dies before Pedro, he will leave the house and the writings to him.” Sounds nothing like a marriage, does it?

❧ ❧ ❧ ❧

Somewhere around the turn of the twelfth century a poem was written, often credited to the Latin poet Hilarius (c.1080- c.1150), also known as Hilary the Englishman, that gushed over the beauty of a “boy of Anjou.” Hilarius was a pupil of Pierre Abélard (c.1079-c.1142), who was a famous poet, philosopher, theologian, and composer. Rumors circulated that Hilarius may have male-love leaning tendencies, which led to Abélard almost dropping him as a student. The earlier mentioned poem was even more proof of Abélard’s suspicions. The poem says, in part, “To a boy in Anjou, Handsome young man, I bow down before you. On bended knee, with fingers entwined.” Not much is known of Hilarius’ later years; his name is seen as a teacher in Angers, France, but there is a chance this is not the same gay, literary genius.

❧ ❧ ❧ ❧

Usually remembered as the absent, crusading, “goodhearted” king in Robin Hood, or by his moniker, Richard the Lionheart; Richard I of England (1157-1199), though religiously problematic, was a bisexual ancestor. He was believed to be a rather good looking, regal man, and at 6’5", he would tower over people even now, but he was never supposed to be king, having been born fourth in line for the throne. That all changed in 1187, when he and his brothers revolted. As a means to strengthen their revolt, Richard I allied himself and fell in love with King Philip II of France (1165-1223). One first-hand account of their infatuation with each other comes from Roger de Hoveden who was a friend of both kings,

> "Richard, [then] duke of Aquitaine, the son of the king of England, remained with Philip, the King of France, who so honored him for so long that they ate every day at the same table and from the same dish, and at night their beds did not separate them. And the king of France loved him as his own soul; and they loved each other so much that the king of England was absolutely astonished by the passionate love between them and marveled at it."

In the end, their love led to both the rise and fall of Richard the Lionheart: he became king, and then after war between their nations broke out, he was killed in battle.

❧ ❧ ❧ ❧

Words evolve over time, both in how they are spelled and defined/ used. Words describing gender are no different. When seen in use from the thirteenth century, the term “**girl**” was used to describe children in general, not simply female-presenting humans, with “knave girl” referring to children assigned male at birth, and “gay girl" for children assigned female at birth. The exact reason the word evolved to only refer to female-identifying humans is not known, but scholars believe that it may be in part due to society's growing association with female-identifying people and concepts like small, innocent, dainty, etc. In line with this evolution of binary gender concepts, children's clothing, up until about 70 years ago, was all unisex (dresses typically, as this was easiest to work with for parents and children alike) until department stores split their children's sections. Even the now standard gendering colors, blue for boys and pink for girls is a new pairing. In 1939 *Parents Magazine* wrote that pink, because it was light red, which is the color of Mars, the god of war, was better for boys; and blue, being associated with Venus and the Madonna, was better for girls. Basically, pink was strong, and blue was delicate, and yet people will argue until their last breath the reverse today. These older color associations and unisex clothing ideal held true through WWII until manufacturing and business strategies shifted, gendering clothing even more, and reassigning the gender-associated colors.

At 20 years old, Jewish philosopher and poet Kalonymus ben Kalonymus (c.1286- c.1330), born with the title of Nasi (biblical Hebrew for prince), began writing and translating on a professional level. Their original works and translations were so incredible that all but one manuscript still exist today. There is one original work that stands out in queer history and that is *Even Bohan*, written in 1322. It was meant to be a commentary on the vices of their contemporaries and themselves, drawing on man's vanity. A part within this work has been suggested to reference Kalonymus' transgender or gay identity and is called the *Prayer for Transformation*. This 11-stanza poem is beautiful, with lines such as, "Woe to me, my mother, that you ever bore a son. What a great loss and no gain! I was created closed-eyed and hardhearted," and "Oh, but had the artisan who made me created me instead – a worthy woman. Today I would be wise and insightful." They go on to speak about the love they would hope to receive,

> "And when I was ready, and the time was right an excellent youth (husband) would be my fortune. He would love me, place me on a pedestal, dress me in jewels of gold earrings, bracelets, necklaces."

In the end of this moving piece, Kalonymus explains their battle with their authentic self and their religious identity,

> "What shall I say? Why cry or be bitter? If my father in heaven has decreed upon me and has maimed me with an immutable deformity, then I do not wish to remove it...I will bless in a voice hushed and weak: blessed are you YHVH who has not made me a woman."

Eleanor Rykener was a bisexual, transfeminine sex worker from England and thanks to her December 1394 arrest, we now have a clear record of her existence. Dressed in female-associated clothing and makeup, presenting overall feminine, and referring to herself as Eleanor, she was caught having sex with a client and was subsequently arrested and interrogated by the mayor of London. This interrogation is memorialized in court documents and outlines Rykener's story. She told of starting out under the wing of Elizabeth Brouderer, learning how to embroider, as well as being taught how to seduce men to obtain the best clients, and most likely being given her name of Rykener, which means 'to reckon' or 'to pay for.' She became quite gifted at both skill sets and traveled all over England for years using these talents. While traveling she had relationships with men and women and was not shy about sharing this with her arresters. When she was arrested and questioned, she was accused of two offences, prostitution and sodomy, but she was not charged with either and was released. The court was quoted as being "unsure as to what to do with" her.

ᘒ ᘒ ᘓ ᘓ

There were different bonding (and binding) rituals performed, like adelphopoiesis for Christian gay men, for other intersectionalities of gay men. Two types of these were affrèrement and matelotage, dating back to at least the 1400s and 1600s, respectively. Affrèrements were common in medieval France and Mediterranean Europe, sometimes used by older people with no heirs to legally leave their possessions, and other times, to bind two men who were in love. The oath that went along with affrèrements was, "un pain, un vin, et une bourse" (one bread, one wine, and one purse), and was meant as a legally binding vow. Matelotage, comparably, was meant to tie two men together in all ways, and in a modern sense, was a pirate marriage where rings were exchanged. Just like with other binding rituals, some matelotages were done specifically for financial or alliance purposes, but others were for the sexual component of relationships too. This latter part is evident from a letter that the governor of Tortuga in the Caribbean, Jean Le Vasseur (d.1653), sent to the French government in 1645. In this letter he requested 2,000 sex workers (assigned female at birth) be sent from the Paris prison system to the island, to curb pirates from entering matelotages. The request was granted but had no real impact on curbing the practice of matelotages. Some pirates left their partnerships, but most did not, some even had a wife join their matelotage as a shared third partner, or throuple; and there is even a book that is said to be a first-hand account of this latter relationship type, *Memoirs of a Buccaneer*, which was published in 1697.

❧ ❧ ☙ ☙

Sun-bin Bong (순빈 봉씨) (c.1414- c.1436) was a princess for half of her life, going by the title Crown Princess Sun of the Haeum Bong Clan while married to the Crown Prince of Joseon, in Korea. Crown Princess Sun was the second wife for the Crown Prince, and when she did not become pregnant right away, he began sleeping with another woman, and in true player fashion, so did Lady Bong. It was rumored she started sleeping with several people, but the individual who stood out was one of her maids, a woman from an enslaved class called nobi, named So-ssang (소쌍). The adultery would have been bad enough for her, but there were laws forbidding the classes from "co-mingling" which set her up harsher sentences. When Lady Bong was accused of her crimes in 1436, besides the accusations of lesbianism and adultery, there were also charges of stealing surpluses of food and clothing and sending it back to her home village to help, which makes her a wealth redistribution icon, but also was considered a crime because she did not ask permission from the prince. She was stripped of the title of Crown Princess, banished from court and left with nothing to her name; after her sentence there is no known trace of Bong's life, though it was typical that women in this position were murdered.

❧ ❧ ☙ ☙

The Renaissance gave the world many of the most well-known artists, from Raphael to Botticelli, but something perhaps less well known about these artists is that almost all of them happened to have queer relationships. For instance, most people learned of Leonardo da Vinci (1452-1519), the Italian mathematician, inventor, painter, and all-around genius, but the lesser-taught part is that he had many gay relationships over the course of his life. He was known to use his lovers as muses, even rumored to have placed them in his works, from *The Last Supper* to his *Saint John the Baptist*. Proof of his exploits are documented in court records from Florence, which show that when he was twenty-four he became one of the 17,000 men in a seventy-year span to be arrested for having sex with another man. Luckily for da Vinci and the world, he was acquitted of the crimes because had he been found guilty the penalty was death, and we never would have had the *Mona Lisa*, *Vitruvian Man*, or any of the rest of his work. Michelangelo (1475-1564), da Vinci's Renaissance equivalent of a frenemy, is most known for his painted works, such as the Sistine Chapel (1508), but a little-taught aspect of his life is the gay love that inspired him. He wrote passionate poetry to his lover, Tommaso Cavalieri (1512-1587), thirty poems in fact, which makes Cavalieri the largest single muse for Michelangelo's art. One of the poems he penned for Cavalieri goes,

> "Perhaps your spirit which sees with greater credence than I dare to believe, the virtuous fire that burns me will be quick to pity me. Oh, happy that day when this be sure to happen, so that I might have my sweet and longed for lord in my unworthy yet ready arms forever."

In 1517, the massive fifty-seven-book work, *Multaqā al-Abhur* (translated to *Confluence of the Seas*) was written by Ibrāhīm ibn Muhammad ibn Ibrāhīm al-Halabī (c.1460- 1549) as a combination of a few earlier Hanafī jurisprudence (legal standards). He included notes on how often the ruling was agreed upon amongst the authorities, and examples of prior cases, which led to his collection becoming a standard reference for legal courts. He made a point to cover as many of the legal situations that could occur as he could, including all the people that could be affected. In his work he included an entire book (book 56) on intersex people in the laws, from how inheritance would work, to using pronouns other than those typically associated with men/women, acknowledging that they exist outside of the binary. Similar laws are seen throughout history, going back in the Western world through Hywel the Good (c.880- c.948), who implemented standards in his laws to include intersex people and the number of variations that the term could include.

Laudomia Forteguerri (c.1515- c.1555) was an Italian lesbian poet known for her charm, beauty, and intellect, in an age when women rarely ever held jobs, let alone knew how to write and read. She is thought to be the first woman whose poetry was discussed in an academic setting, which in 1541 was extremely risky based on the subject of the works. Forteguerri was born to a wealthy family in

Siena, Italy, and was married twice, but neither of those marriages sparked her passion quite like Margaret of Parma (1522-1586), and it was for her that Forteguerri wrote her famed poetry. One of the five sonnets she wrote for Margaret goes, "listen to my words, how they are ready, to beseech you. Nor do I want anything else, but that you keep me close to my goddess." If her poetry was not obvious enough, Alessandro Piccolomini, the "friend" who discussed and published her work without telling her, openly spoke in his lecture and book about the women meeting and instantly falling in love. Forteguerri was more than a Sappho-inspired writer, she is also remembered for being a fierce warrior. In 1554, after decades of battling with Spanish occupying forces, the people of Siena decided to revolt even though their survival chances were low. The revolt meant that every individual person of their small republic needed to act. Forteguerri led a group of 1,000 women to build fortifications to protect the territory. Though courageous, it was to no avail, and she is presumed to have died in the ensuing year-and-a-half-long battle.

The king that Guy Fawkes had the Gunpowder (treason and) Plot to blow up in 1605, the James in colonial Jamestown, VA, and the King James of the King James Bible, are all one man, and a rather hypocritically flamboyant one at that, King James I of England (1566-1625). During his reign, England and Scotland were united under one rule for the first time in centuries, England began to colonize the Americas, and harsh punishments for queer sex continued (originating from Henry VIII's Buggery Act of 1533). James I was known to have had multiple affairs with men in his life, two of the most remembered are with Robert Carr (c.1587-1645) and George Villiers (1592-1628). To start, James I knighted both men, and gifted them with clothes, horses, land, and titles (1st Earl of Somerset and 1st Duke of Buckingham, accordingly). Carr was one of the king's first real loves; he fell in love with him after watching Carr in a jousting match. Carr was injured, and the king came running to nurse him back to health. During their romance,

Carr even poisoned a rival: everyone in court knew, but the king pardoned him, which led to Carr's having even more rivals. After years together there was a falling out in 1616, with treason and the like, but King James I could not kill his beloved, and just had him locked in London Tower for a few years (what a guy). Villiers came to the King's attention in 1615, because Carr's rivals wanted it that way, and it worked. Sir John Oglander (1585-1655) once wrote,

> "never yet saw any fond husband make so much or so great dalliance over his beautiful spouse as I have seen King James over his favourites, especially the Duke of Buckingham."

King James I even made a secret stairwell in the wall of the palace from his room to Villiers'. His rivals would taunt, "Elizabeth was a king, and now James is a queen," a reference to his predecessor, Queen Elizabeth I.

❧ ❧ ❧ ❧

The existence of Eleno de Céspedes' (c.1545- *after* 1588) story is another one for which we have court documents to "thank," in this case, the Spanish Inquisition in 1587. Céspedes was most likely a trans or intersex man, given the details that are known from his trial. He was born to a Black Muslim woman who was enslaved, and a white Christian man who was free, and because of this he was raised as an enslaved human at the beginning of his life. Once he was freed with limited options to survive, he married a man named Cristóbal Lombardo and was pregnant by 16. Céspedes said that after giving birth his external sex characteristics changed, his husband abandoned him, he left his son with family, got into a scuffle with a pimp named Heredia, whom he stabbed, and then he began to travel all over Spain. During his travels he fell in love with María del Caño, and they were to marry in December 1584. The priest at the wedding decided he was not sure about Céspedes' gender since he did not have facial hair and called for a physician's examination, to which the doctor came back declaring Céspedes a male. For a little over two years, the couple were happily married, until neighbors reported them to the Inquisition and the couple was arrested on charges of sodomy (which was used in general for acts deemed "unnatural" sex crimes). Céspedes was charged with pretending to be a man, using witchcraft to trick the doctors, mocking the "sanctity" of marriage, and numerous other items. The tribunal argued that Céspedes was always a "woman," but he brought forth numerous witnesses to attest to his being a man, from lovers to doctors. The trial was messy and lasted years, and nearing the end there was said to be an injury and potential amputation, and now the doctors observed only female-assigned sex characteristics; basically, not wanting to deal with the disaster and fallout, he was only found guilty of bigamy, for not properly divorcing his first spouse. He was sentenced to 200 lashes, and community service, and became somewhat of a local celebrity.

MAL CUT PURSE.

See here the Preſideſſe o'th pilfring Trade
Mercuryes ſecond: Venus's onely Mayd
Doublet and breeches in a Uniform dreſſe
the Female Humurriſt a Kickſhaw meſſe
Here no attraction that your fancy greets
But if her FEATURES pleaſe not read her FEATS.

London Published 1793. by J. Caulfield.

Etching and poem of Moll Cutpurse remade in 1793
from the 1600s original.

Chapter Two: Truly Vers- Ruling Queers to Drag Queens (1600-1899)

Mary Frith aka Moll (or Mal) Cutpurse aka Tom Faconer (c.1584-1659) was one of the OG's in seventeenth century London, and she happens to be a woman. She wore pants, drank and smoked in public, stole, was a pimp, and had multiple plays written about her (even while she was still alive); she truly lived an iconic life. Firth was arrested numerous times for all the aforementioned 'crimes,' including the pants and play ones, since at one of the performances she drank and cursed on stage and was arrested. It was one of those arrests that in 1600 got her noticed, catapulting her into local fame and myth. She was known always to do as she pleased, including in her sexual relations, and enjoyed putting on a show of remorse, only to be released, brag and commit her crimes again. Her nickname Moll (Mal) Cutpurse can be broken down to pretty much sum up her reputation; Moll (or Mal) was a term used to describe "deplorable" women of the time, and "cutpurse" was another word for thief. The engraving pictures that remain of her show a rugged looking woman, usually smoking a pipe in a tricorn hat.

When the English created their first permanent settlement in America at Jamestown, queer family was there. Their name was Thomas (born Thomasine) Hall (c.1603- *after* 1629). Hall's story is told in their own words, due to an uproar that occurred in 1628. They were able to move to Jamestown as an indentured servant, a position they obtained while presenting male. After a brief stay there, they moved to Warrosquyoacke, a small village also in Virginia; but while living and becoming comfortable, Hall often wore women's clothes in public, causing a stir in the community. Adding fuel to the fire was the fact that when questioned about why they would wear clothing associated with multiple genders, Hall alluded to the fact that it was not just because they wanted to, but also for sex. They ended up being arrested because it was said that their changing of dress, and the fact they were intimate with men and women, was causing "disorder" in the village (note: they had to have been hooking up with someone, and Warrosquyoacke was a village of only 200 people). In 1629, after months of back and forth, and numerous physical exams, the court decided to just have Hall, "goe clothed in man's apparell, only his head to bee attired in a coyfe and croscloth with an apron before him." Basically, they were made to always wear male and female clothing.

❧ ❧ ❧ ❧

Typically recognized as the slightly timid monarch from Alexandre Dumas' 1844 classic, *The Three Musketeers*, King Louis XIII of

France (1601-1643) was most certainly queer. Not only did he have multiple male lovers, and openly avoided having intercourse with his wife, but he also introduced wigs into high (court) fashion in 1624, and it does not get more fundamentally gay than that. As we all should, Louis XIII had deal-breakers, and when one of his favorite lovers, or mignons as they were called, François de Baradas took part in a duel, after the King had outlawed them, Baradas almost immediately fell out of favor. Into Baradas' place stepped Henri Coiffier de Ruzé, Marquis of Cinq-Mars (c.1620-1642). In reference to Louis XIII's affection for Ruzé, French writer Gédéon Tallemant (1619-1692) noted one time when the King sent the Marquis to undress and,

> "Who returned, adorned like a bride. 'To bed, to bed' he said to him impatiently... and the mignon was not in before the king was already kissing his hands."

Though as with his other paramours, the King was unlucky in love, and after time Ruzé betrayed him, and was arrested and executed for treason. Where Louis XIII was successful was in suppressing revolts, eliminating private armies held by aristocrats, which effectively consolidated power to the throne, setting up his son, Louis XIV, to be the most powerful monarch in French history. Louis XIV separately, was not a fan of gay relationships and ended up exiling a number of aristocrats, including his own son, for being members of a secret gay brotherhood.

☙ ☙ ❧ ❧

In 1632, her father, Gustavus Adolphus, died in battle, and so, at six years old, Christina (1626-1689) from the House of Vasa, became Christina, Queen of Sweden. She was the only heir, so she was given an education that was typically only given to princes, and excelled wildly, learning to speak eight languages in her lifetime. She was known for her signature tangled hair, never using makeup, and wearing men's clothes; the reason for this was that she believed, if she had time to "get ready," then she had time to read and educate herself, which is a fair point when you consider the amount of time that went into seventeenth-century fashion. Christina bragged about her sexual escapades, particularly about her relationship with Ebba Sparre (c.1629-1662), who she introduced to court as her "bedfellow," and was once said to comment on Sparre, "her intellect is as striking as her body." Even though Christina was an able ruler, it was not how she envisioned her life, particularly the control and marriage part of it. At twenty-three, she announced that she had decided to never marry, nor have children, and she named her cousin as her heir, and besides the nobles, most of the country was quite accepting of this. When she was twenty-eight (with twenty-two years as queen), Christina abdicated the throne and moved to Rome to immerse herself in the world of theater and art. She continued to write to Sparre, but was never able to see her again, as Sparre's family prevented them from meeting. While in Rome she did have a few flings, two being with singer Angelina Giorgino and

French aristocrat, Gabrielle de Rochechouart de Mortemart. Pope Alexander VII remarked that Christina was “a queen without a realm, a Christian without faith, and a woman without shame." She is also one of the only women to be buried in the Vatican Grotto at St. Peter's Basilica.

The first (and potentially only) criminal conviction during the colonial period in America for lesbian behavior in the "New World" occurred on October 2, 1650, in the Plymouth colony, what is now Massachusetts. The trial began in March of 1648, and the defendants were Sarah White Norman (c.1625-1654) and Mary Vincent Hammon (c.1633-1705). Their specific crimes were, "lewd behavior with each other upon a bed." The charges were brought against them by a neighbor named Richard Berry, whose name was later seen in court documents for a similar crime "upon a bed" with a man, alluding to the fact that he most likely turned the women in to save himself. In the end, Hammon was let go with a warning, most likely based on her age, while Norman, who was married with children at the time, had to publicly acknowledge her "unchaste behavior," in somewhat of a *Scarlet Letter* scenario.

What started as an underground network of Black Magic, midwifery, abortion assistance, fortune telling, and the occasional "inheritance potion" (aka poison), turned into a plot to commit regicide against King Louis XIV, and led to more than 200 arrests. At the center of L'Affaire des Poisons, or the Poisons Affair, was Catherine Monvoisin or La Voisin (c.1640-1680) and her fortune-telling business partners, Catherine Trianon (c.1627-1681) and La Doddée (who was Trianon's romantic partner). The three women were main players in the beginning of the five-year poisoning and

Black Magic ring that ran in Paris, France from 1677-1682. For these three, it all came to a head when Madame de Montespan enlisted them for the ultimate murder, that of King Louis XIV. Trianon is said to have attempted to back out, but it was too late; she was linked to the plot and when it was discovered they were all arrested to be tried for treason. Monvoisin was executed, Trianon died by suicide before they could fully interrogate her, and it is unknown what happened to La Doddée.

❧ ❧ ❧ ❧

Most people know that prior to the word "**gay**" referencing male-male attraction, or even queer people as a whole, it simply meant "happy," but before that, it had another meaning. In the early eighteenth century, "gay" was used to reference things/people that were thought to be "addicted to pleasures and dissipations," or "uninhibited by moral constraints." To explain in use: a gay house was a brothel, a gay man/woman meant sex worker or at times, promiscuous. This idea of being "uninhibited" or effectively "free" then evolved to mean happy, and from there it was reclaimed by the queer community, because we are happy, and free, and uninhibited.

❧ ❧ ❧ ❧

After the Glorious Revolution of 1688, there was a shift in England from relatively socially liberal to staunchly conservative, and with that came the forming of the Society for the Reformation of Manners. This society was essentially the fun police: their goal was to suppress all profanity, immorality (in their eyes), sex work, and "lewd" acts/places in general. One of the types of "lewd" places the Society went after were molly houses. These "houses" were congregating spots for gay men, usually coffee shops, pubs, or little

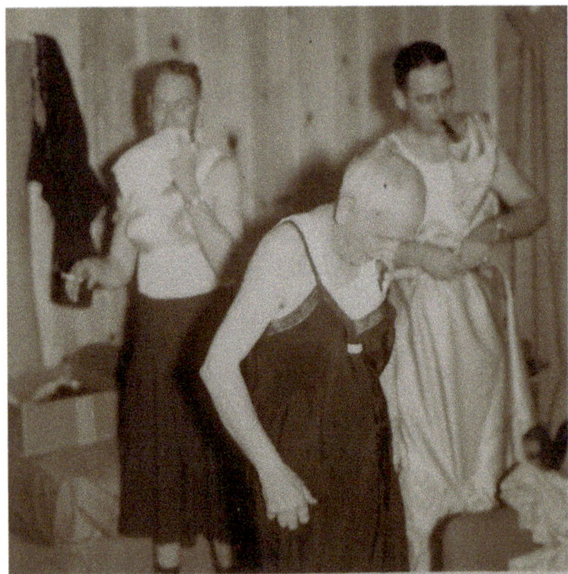

(Left and below) Getting ready for a drag show c. 1950

hotels, and were called such because "molly" was a slang term for gay men at the time ("tommy" was a slang term for a lesbian). One of the most well-known molly houses was Margaret "Mother" Clap's house. Clap was not known to be queer herself but was a fierce ally. Besides running a molly house, she was known to have given false testimony on occasion to get her customers out of arrests. Her house was open from 1724-1726, closing after a former patron turned informant in order to avoid a death sentence. The informant, Thomas Newton, went on record about his own sexuality in court, describing several of his sexual encounters with men. And though he stated, "I think there's no Crime in making what use I please of my own Body," his information led to the raid in February 1726 and forty people being arrested, including Clap, who was sentenced to two years in prison. She was charged with running a brothel and encouraging "Persons to commit Sodomy," and from the Old Bailey records, details of her molly house are found. One of the patrons who testified against her described the multiple rooms in her house where "marriages" would take place, and went into detail about the normal scene there each night,

> "Near Men Fifty there, making Love to one another as they call'd it. Sometimes they'd sit in one anothers Laps, use their Hands indecently Dance and make Curtsies and mimick the Language of Women."

The Society focused so much on the erasure of queer meeting

places, that by the 1730s, molly houses were all but gone, and it took more than two decades for them to start to appear again.

❧ ❧ ☙ ☙

Chevalière d'Éon (1728-1810) is a trans icon who transcends time and speaks to the notion that it's never too late to start being yourself. Assigned male at birth, and predominantly presenting that way for forty-nine years, d'Éon was an accomplished soldier and spy. She was a member of King Louis XV Secret du Roi (translated to King's Secret), which was a confidential group of spies that worked personally for the King. This came in handy when, in 1763, a rival showed up in court and threatened her place, but because of all the secrets she knew, she was able to escape and live in exile until it was safe to return. When she did finally return to France in 1777, she presented as female; and in true legend fashion, anytime anyone questioned her gender, she exclaimed that she had always been female, and they were all wrong the whole time. Some people were suspicious, but given her extraordinary reputation, very few bothered her. Though her last decade or so was spent in and out of poverty, she was able to live the last thirty-three years of her life as her authentic self.

❧ ❧ ☙ ☙

Growing up with a homophobic parent is never pleasant, and that is even more true when your parent is the King of Prussia and literally has the legal ability to murder your partners; this was the reality for

Frederick the Great (1712-1786). His father was Frederick William I of Prussia (1688-1740), known as the "Soldier King," and he held a hyper-masculine court. Though Frederick the Great was a superior military strategist, his effeminate nature made him stand out in this type of atmosphere. At sixteen, he fell in love with one of his father's pages, Peter Karl van Keith, and when his father noticed, he had Keith sent to the front lines of battle to perish. Two years later, Frederick fell in love again, this time with a fellow soldier, Hans Hermann von Katte. They plotted to escape Frederick William I's rule and run off together, but their plan was foiled. Frederick's father had Katte executed for treason and made Frederick watch. Frederick's only saving grace at home was his older sister, Princess Wilhelmine (1709-1758), who was his most trusted confidante. When, at twenty-one, he was forced to marry, it was his sister whom he turned to and confided about how he would rather die than marry a woman. Though he always showed his wife respect, he did everything he could to avoid her at all costs, even moving her into her own palace and seeing her only once a year, on her birthday. Frederick kept his own home, one filled with custom commissioned homoerotic art, and always with men. Under Frederick the Great's rule, Prussia thrived, and he made it possible for common men to run for government positions and sit as judges, which was a huge step for democratic systems. He was also a brilliant military leader, expanding the territories of Prussia, but he faced defeat at times.

After one such moment he penned a letter that read in part, “fortune has it in for me, she is a woman, and I am not that way inclined.”

Even though LGBTQIA+ people were (and are) part of the typical landscape of society, the punishment for being caught engaging in queer acts was (and in many countries still is) death. In France, Jean Diot (c.1710-1750) and Bruno Lenoir (c.1727-1750) were the last two men to be executed by the government for simply being attracted to one another. On January 4, 1750, the two men were caught engaging in what the night watchman deemed "indecent and reprehensible" behavior, and they were immediately arrested. After months of sitting in jail, on May 27 they were found guilty and sentenced to die by burning at the stake, which was promptly carried out. A little over forty years later, France adopted the Penal Code of 1791, which, unlike prior laws, made no mention of queer lives in private, so it "decriminalized" consenting, adult queer sex, making France the first Western country to do so. When the code was introduced, it was intended to prosecute only "true crimes" and not fabricated offenses only supported by "superstition."

❧ ❧ ❧ ❧

Some of the events that occurred throughout history truly feel like they are ripped from a *Maury* show topic list, and the case of Princess Isabella of Parma (1741-1763) and her love affair with Archduchess Maria Christina (1742-1798) is no different. Isabella was eighteen when she married Maria Christina's brother, and from the beginning she was not pleased at all. Though Joseph II, Holy Roman Emperor (1741-1790) showered her with love, it was his sister, Maria Christina, from whom she could not part. In the three years they spent at court together, they were nearly inseparable, and in the rare moments they were apart, they wrote letters, more than 200 to be exact. Most of those surviving were letters Isabella kept, as the ones Maria Christina had in her possession were destroyed by her family after her death. In one letter Isabella writes,

> "I am told that the day begins with God. I, however, begin the day by thinking of the object of my love, for I think of her incessantly."

They were often referred to as Orpheus and Eurydice, the ill-fated Greek lovers who followed each other into Hades, and like those lovers, Isabella and Maria Christina's love was cut short when at the age of twenty-one, Isabella passed away after giving birth to a stillborn baby.

❧ ❧ ❧ ❧

In a room full of interesting people, the Public(k) Universal Friend (c.1752-1819) would probably be hard to beat out for the top spot. Assigned female at birth, the Universal Friend was born to Quaker parents in Rhode Island and was raised in the faith (the Quakers call themselves the Religious Society of Friends). In October 1776, they suffered some kind of fit or illness, after which they said that "Jemima Wilkinson had died and her soul ascended to heaven," and that God with the help of some Archangels transformed their body into a genderless being, named Public Universal Friend, whose mission it was to be a prophet, so to speak. They began wearing androgynous or masculine associated clothing and requested to no longer be referred to by male or female pronouns. They traveled the New England area preaching and founded their own religious offshoot of Quakerism called Society of Universal Friends, which makes it the first American-founded religion (this is specifically about colonial America, not the land itself and Indigenous people). The Friend preached humility, hospitality, and was a fierce opponent of slavery, actively convincing their followers and others to free the people they enslaved. They also in turn invited those newly freed people to join their flock and would feed and house anyone who needed it. By 1790, they had gathered enough followers to found a settlement in upstate New York called Jerusalem. Over the years, followers came and went, and The Friend faced adversity based on their beliefs and appearance, having to disappear via their skilled horse riding on more than one occasion. The religion they created, on the other hand, did not just disappear and lasted beyond their passing in 1819. There are records of the Society of Universal Friends through the 1860s.

An unemployed gay Prussian soldier is credited with building the Continental Army and helping America win the Revolutionary War. Friedrich Wilhelm von Steuben (1730-1794) started his military career under another gay legend, Frederick the Great, and rose to captain, before being "demobilized," basically let go, in 1763. Steuben held various minor titles in Germany, searching for a chance to lead an army again, but was denied by multiple countries. In 1777, he finally had his chance when an emerging nation (the United States) was revolting, and they did not have a trained standing army. With the help of the French Minister of War (Count de St. Germain) Steuben traveled to the colonies and met with General George Washington, who immediately put him in charge to set the rules and organize training for the Army. Steuben wrote the *Regulations for the Order and Discipline of the Troops of the United States*, the standard training guide that turned the inexperienced colonists into soldiers. He never married, and the reason is noted in many correspondences: he was said to have "intense emotional relationships" with a number of men. The two relationships that meant that most to Steuben were with Capt. Benjamin Walker (1753-1818) and William North, both of whom were left Steuben's estate when he died.

❧ ❧ ❧ ❧

One of the first doctors to successfully perform a c-section in which both the birthing parent and child survived (the child being named after him), was Dr. James Barry (c.1789-1865), who happened to be a transgender man. Born in Ireland and assigned female at birth, Barry began presenting male publicly around 1809, and applied to medical school, where he successfully graduated and then joined the army to serve as a surgeon. He was stationed in Cape Town, South Africa where he worked hard to improve sanitation, living conditions and water quality, not only for the soldiers, but for the local people as well. Barry rose through the ranks of the British military, traveling the world and bettering the places he went, from South Africa to Canada. He was known to always be vocal, sometimes aggressive, in fighting for underprivileged and underserved communities. The public was unaware of the sex he was assigned at birth until he died, and people began to talk about his autopsy. Barry was very well respected, however, and Major McKinnon, the man who signed his death certificate was quoted as saying that whether Barry was assigned male or female at birth was "none of my business," (which is a great example of how sex assigned at birth should be treated).

☙ ☙ ❧ ❧

Many people keep diaries, but very few become published diarists. Anne Lister (1791-1840) is one of those few. The published diary (*The Secret Diaries of Miss Anne Lister*, 2010) is only a partial version, and that is directly related to the original work being over 5,000,000 words. To put into context just how many words that is, the longest *Lord of the Rings* book was only 177,227 words, or roughly 3.5% of Lister's word count. The reason for the length was directly related to Lister writing consistent diaries, detailing everything in her life from the weather, to politics, to her personal love life, for thirty-four years. The diary began in 1806, a little after she was sent to the Manor House School in York, England, and developed her first relationship, with a fellow student, Eliza Raine (c.1793- 1860). The two love birds created a secret code that they would write in so that could pass notes undetected, and this is the code that Lister would use for the parts of her diary that involved her world-traveling lesbian escapades. When the code was finally cracked by her nephew after her death, people thought it was a hoax because of how explicitly detailed it was. The dairy was in fact real and led to Lister's being called "the first modern lesbian." Lister detailed all her dalliances, from her schoolgirl trysts to the women she romanced in France, Belgium, Germany, and Switzerland, all leading to her falling in love and "marrying" Ann Walker (1803-1854). The wedding Lister described was not one of legal recognition but was nevertheless real to the two of them. On March 30, 1834, they took communion together at the Holy Trinity Church in Goodramgate, York, and referred to themselves as wedded partners thereafter. Lister's "jet-setting" lifestyle did not slow down with marriage, because in Walker she found a companion to join her, and for six years they traveled Europe together, until Lister passed away. The show *Gentleman Jack* on HBO is based on her life and work, and a full version of Lister's diary is available for free online and includes photographs.

☙ ☙ ❧ ❧

The term United Kingdom refers to England, Scotland, Wales, and Northern Ireland, and it exists because of 1800's *An Act for the Union of Great Britain and Ireland*, which was passed in large part due to Robert Stewart, Viscount Castlereagh (1769-1822), a queer politician. Stewart was born into a landowning, political family in Ireland, which set him up for a life of relative success. In his civil career, he held titles from Chief Secretary for Ireland to leader of the British House of Commons, and as with most politicians, it led to his not being the most liked man of his time. Though he was married, and by all accounts cared very much for his wife, in the last year of his life he was being blackmailed for having secret affairs with men. He went so far as to confide in King George III that he was accused of "the same crimes as Bishop of Clogher," a priest charged with engaging in an affair with a soldier in the back of a tavern. Days after the meeting with the king, Stewart died by suicide, but this act caused a butterfly effect for the future of natural science. Stewart's nephew was Robert FitzRoy, and when he was put in command of the HMS *Beagle*, he feared being alone and potentially becoming depressed like his uncle, so he requested a companion for the voyage, someone who enjoyed science and research. The man he got was Charles Darwin, and so the world received Darwin's theories on evolution and *On the Origin of Species*.

Nestled in the middle of Vermont is a tiny town named Weybridge, where in 1807, lesbian and seamstress, Charity Bryant (1777-1851) planned a short visit with a friend, but met the love of her life, Sylvia Drake (1784-1868), and ended up staying for the remaining forty-four years of her life. Bryant was a world-traveling woman of fashion and a known lesbian, but rumors had started; in fact, this was one of the reasons she decided to vacation in a town with a population of approximately 510 people. She met Drake, the younger sister of her friend, right after she arrived, and knew immediately they were each other's future. Bryant opened a business making clothing for the townspeople, and hired Drake as her assistant, which provided a perfect cover for the large amount of private time they would spend together. Within months, Bryant had asked Drake to move into a one-bedroom home together, which they celebrated as their "wedding" anniversary. In letters and diaries written by the two women, as well as items from relatives and neighbors, Bryant and Drake are acknowledged as life partners. One of their neighbors, Hiram Harvey Hurlburt, wrote in his diary of the couple, "I heard it mentioned as if Miss Bryant and Miss Drake were married to each other." He then went on to say, "Miss Bryant was the man, this I thought was perfectly proper." If all of this wasn't proof enough, when Drake died, she had them buried under one headstone in a Weybridge cemetery, to be together forever.

❧ ❧ ❧ ❧

A little over 200 years after his birth, Andreas Bruce's (1808-1885) life story was published. Largely told in his own words through letters and writings, the release of *Therese Andreas Bruce* in 2013,

made Bruce's story one of the oldest confirmed first-hand accounts of transgender lives in the Western world. Born in Sweden, and assigned female at birth, Bruce preferred to present masculine from early childhood, even having the nickname of "Fröken Herrn" or "Miss Master" because he would always join in with his brothers in their activities. At sixteen, after being forced to dress in female clothing by his parents, he cut his hair, ran away, and left a note that threatened suicide. Completely distraught at the potential of losing their child, his parents brought him to the doctor, where Bruce said, "If I cannot live in trousers, then I cannot live at all." The doctor took this seriously and pronounced Bruce intersex with sex characteristics more male presenting, which would allow him to legally present male in public. Though at first his father was supportive, even giving him the name of Andreas, when people in the town began to talk, the family disowned Bruce. He moved and joined the military for a short time, and worked on ships, where he was known to be one of the hardest workers among the crew. In 1838, Bruce became pregnant as a result of what was most likely a sexual assault, and had a daughter named Carolina. At first this was a dark period for him, but after meeting Maria Lindblad, he grew to be a family man. Lindblad and Bruce raised his daughter, and hers, as mother and father, creating one of the first "everyday" modern families.

☙ ☙ ❧ ❧

In January of 1810, a molly house named The White Swan opened, and with the return of molly houses came the raids, this time by the first "professional" police force in London, the Bow Street Runners. The White Swan was raided only six months after it opened, and the raid led to a group of men, nicknamed the Vere Street Coterie, to be arrested, and ultimately two being hanged. Much of the history comes from Robert Holloway's 71 page, *The Phoenix of Sodom; Or, the Vere Street Coterie* (1813), which is a firsthand interview with James Cook, the proprietor of The White Swan (it also contains other details and little-known events that truly are quintessential queer history). In Cook's own words, he tells the story of how he was approached by a man named Yardley about becoming partners in a Public House for a specific clientele. Yardley promised he knew, "great number of gentlemen, some hundreds" that could and would frequent the establishment and pay well. Apparently, Yardley knew a man who had done this and was able to retire in three years, so Cook agreed. They rented a space on Vere Street, and set up The White Swan, which was a space with multiple rooms, one of them described in *The Phoenix* as,

> "Called the Chaple, where marriages took place, sometimes between a female grenadier, six feet high, and a petit maitre not more than half the altitude of his beloved wife! These marriages were solemnized with all the mockery of bride maids and bride men."

In this scene he is describing marriages where the bride and groom were both assigned male at birth. Holloway even wrote in shock, of some of the drag names the patrons would use in juxtaposition with their daytime jobs. He said they,

> "Assume feigned names, though not very appropriate to their calling in life: for instance, Kitty Cambric is a Coal Merchant; Miss Selina, Runner at a Police office; Black-eyed Leonora, a Drummer; Pretty Harriet, a Butcher; Lady Godina, a Waiter; the Duchess of Gloucester, a gentleman's servant; Duchess of Devonshire, a Blacksmith; and Miss Sweet Lips, a Country Grocer."

Shocking that Lady Bunny (b.1962, Wigstock co-founder) isn't on this roster of old queens (said in jest, of course). *The Phoenix of Sodom*, though written from the perspective of a person with conservative views on sexuality (even though "doth protest too much, methinks"), he was also an attorney, and the book was meant to garner leniency for Cook, so he included several previous cases and queer accounts, making it a trove of little-heard queer history.

❧ ❧ ❧ ❧

When Mary Jones (1803-*after* 1847) showed up for her appearance in court in 1836, it was the talk of multiple New York newspapers, and it was not just because of her crimes of grand larceny. Jones is pictured in a lithograph as rather beautiful, dressed in a large floral hoop skirt and pearl-colored gloves, in complete contrast with the transphobic caption below, and that was the spark of the articles. An army veteran and sex worker, Jones was arrested on Bleecker St. in NYC, after being accused of robbing multiple clients, and then propositioning a police officer. Adding an additional layer to the offenses was the fact that the clients were white, and Jones was Black. All of this makes the first trans/gender diverse person to present as their authentic self in a United States courtroom, a Black, transfeminine sex worker. When asked during the trial why they wore female presenting clothing, Jones responded in part, “I have always attended parties among the people of my own Colour dressed in this way... and in New Orleans I always dressed in this way.” They ended up being sentenced to five years in prison, but even being locked up could not stifle who they were. There are articles in 1845-46 that cover a person named “Pete Sevanley,” who was arrested multiple times for committing the same crimes, with the identical M.O. as Jones, whose birth name was Pete Sewally (it was commonly known that papers would misspell names and addresses).

❧ ❧ ☙ ☙

The Little Mermaid is a classic fairy tale, having been remade countless times, and yet very few are aware that Hans Christian Andersen (1805-1875) wrote the work to tell the story of how the love of his life, Edvard Collin (1808-1886), was marrying another (he even mailed the story to Collin). This may be confusing, as most people only know the story from Disney's version. A quick, spoiler overview of the original work: Ariel, the mermaid, will live for 300 years and then turn to seafoam (as is standard for mermaids in the tale). When she travels to the ocean surface for the first time she sees the prince drowning, saves him, and immediately falls in love. She learns that humans only live for a limited time, but that they will go to “heaven” to live forever due to their soul. So, to be with her prince, Ariel trades her voice for legs, but every step feels like walking on shards of glass, an allegory for Andersen’s bisexuality of which he could never speak, which caused him pain, but pain he was willing to take to be near his "prince." As the story goes, the prince needed to marry Ariel, or she would become seafoam at midnight, but turns out the prince fell in love with another and Ariel’s fate was just about sealed. She was given one chance to kill her beloved in order to gain her own soul, but Ariel could not go through with it. In the end, her decision to sacrifice herself granted her the chance to be an angel-type character and do good deeds for 300 years and then earn the right to be in “heaven.” There are many connections in the work to Andersen’s life, such as: the love interest picking someone else, written immediately following Collin’s engagement news, the main character being an outsider who longed to be a “part of their world,” plus the literal silence around his love and affection for men. He even wrote in a letter to Collin, “Our friendship is like 'The Mysteries', it should not be analyzed," and "I long for you as though you were a beautiful Calabrian girl." Andersen was known to write his elaborate fairy tales based on the situations in his life. He wrote *The Ugly Duckling* about himself growing up and becoming a celebrated writer, and his work, *The*

Nightingale, was for famed opera singer Jenny Lind (1820-1887), who was nicknamed the Swedish Nightingale (portrayed in the 2017 film, *The Greatest Showman*). As with Collin, this love was not reciprocated, and Lind referred to Andersen as her brother. Another queer nod to *The Little Mermaid* is that Disney animators used photos of the drag queen who starred in John Waters' cult films (ie. *Hairspray* and *Pink Flamingos)*, the legendary, Divine (1945-1988) to make the character Ursula.

One of the oldest laws (in this case ordinance, which just means law on the local level) in the United States that was directly meant to target LGBTQIA+ people and how we presented, came into effect in Columbus, OH in 1848. Where prior laws that were used to police the attire and presentation of people contained general terms such as New York's 1845 law that stated, "painted, discolored, covered, or concealed" faces were not allowed, Columbus' specifically banned appearing in public, "in a dress not belonging to his or her sex." These were the beginnings of a widespread passing of anti-LGBTQIA+ laws, a little over a decade later, in 1863, even the now-queer friendly San Francisco passed the same Columbus ordinance. This has persisted in the US (and numerous other nations) since. Examples include Detroit's 1944 anti-trans/queer ordinance 39-1-35, which stated that people assigned male at birth could not appear in public, or even private premises in the "dress of the opposite sex." Miami's City Ordinance 5521 from 1965, which was an addition to the original 1952 rule that was directly aimed at trans women and drag queens due to the large gay community in the area, and stated that a person could not go out "in a dress not customarily worn by his or her sex," and Delcambre, LA's 2007 archaic ordinance that banned "opposite sex attire" for anyone and everyone, though the author is not sure how they could possibly enforce this.

❧ ❧ ☙ ☙

The Gold Rush of 1849 brought approximately 90,000 people to California, and two of those people were loving couple, John Chaffee (1823-1903) and Jason Chamberlain (1821-1903). The men met in 1846 while in Massachusetts, and bonded quickly, becoming inseparable. Three years later, when the gold rush occurred, they

made the decision to leave all they had ever known and take the almost 200-day trip around Cape Horn in South America, and head to their future in the Indigenous land that would become California. After living and working in San Francisco for four years, they finally decided to take a chance on mining, and moved to Second Garrotte in Toulumne County. It was here that they truly settled into themselves, building their own home, and running an inn for travelers. They were well loved and respected in the community, even mentioned in the 1901 *Illustrated History of Toulumne County,* which besides referring to them as the "first citizens of Second Garrotte" also called them, "bosom companions and partners." The guestbook to their inn is another place where their relationship is noted, though partially in euphemism. It says, "the artistic inclination of these gentlemen, is quite apparent, though which one is the 'ladies' man' we could not discover, each modestly declining the honor." The men stayed together for over fifty years, until Chaffee fell ill and passed away in July of 1903; in October of that same year Chamberlain died by suicide, not being able to handle life without his partner.

❧ ❧ ❧ ❧

James Buchanan (1791-1868) was the only lifelong bachelor President of the United States, and he also happens to be one of the few that were most likely queer. Buchanan spent his life in law and politics: he held his first public office at just twenty-three years old

and continued to climb until he reached the pinnacle of US political aspirations, becoming the 15th President. Where he was successful in his career, he wasn't so much in his public romantic pursuits. When he was twenty-seven, he met and became engaged to the daughter of a wealthy iron manufacturer, but by the time he was twenty-eight he was single again. The couple rarely spent time together, and rumors circulated that not only was Buchanan stepping out on his bride-to-be, but he was only marrying her for her fortune. The engagement was called off and his fiancé passed away months later, which Buchanan used for the rest of his life as his reason not to be intimate with women. He is, however, believed to have had a male partner after the death of his fiancée, and that man was William Rufus King (1786-1853). King was a politician himself, serving as the Vice President for the last year of his life. The two men met in 1840 and proceeded to live together for the next thirteen years, until King's death. Among DC insiders, King was referred to as Buchanan's "better half", "wife", and "Aunt Nancy," the latter term used at the time to reference men considered flamboyant. It is believed, as was common, that letters and items detailing the depth of their love were destroyed, as correspondences are missing in the sequence. What remains still clearly outlines a relationship deeper than that of a hetero friendship, particularly with accounts from colleagues of the men. As a queer coincidence in names, one of the sons of William the Conqueror (c.1028-1087) went by the name William Rufus (c.1060-1100). His title was King, he was never married, kept a court of "pretty men," and was denied a proper burial due to his relationships with those men.

❧ ❧ ❧ ❧

Though the word "soldier" is often synonymous with cismales, there are plenty of women (cis and trans) and transmen who would often take up the cause to fight for their respective nations or beliefs. Irish-born Albert D. J. Cashier (1843-1915) happens to be one of those transmen that decided to fight. Cashier gave interviews in his later life retelling the details of his experience, explaining how he presented male from an early age, and at nineteen made the decision to enlist in the Union Army and fight in the Civil War. He saw more than forty battles in his military career, and was even captured at one point, but managed to escape. He was honorably discharged at the end of the war in 1865 and continued with his authentic life. He lived a quiet life, never having to deal with much adversity, due in large part to no one's being aware that he was a trans individual. That is, until 1914 when he fell ill and was taken to a hospital where they physically examined his body and then forced him to wear women's clothing. To further add to this transphobic treatment, the hospital also reported him to the Veterans' board, who in turn stripped Cashier of his benefits. People were in his corner though, and fellow soldiers came forward in his defense, stating he was in fact the man who fought beside them, and eight months before he died, his benefits and pension were reinstated. He was buried in his uniform, and given full military honors, including his name, rank, and military company engraved on his headstone.

❧ ❧ ❧ ❧

When Karl Heinrich Ulrichs (1825-1895) became the first person in the sphere of the Western world to come out publicly, he did so to fight for the repeal of anti-gay laws in Germany. On August 29,1867, Ulrichs passionately fought for the love that he felt, and said, "I am proud, that I found the courage to deal the initial blow to

Non-cismale Civil War era soldier

the hydra of public contempt." Although he was yelled off the podium, this defiant act did in fact lead to a chain reaction of activism. It all began five years earlier when Ulrichs came out to his family, and one of the difficulties he faced in understanding who he was, was the lack of clear language around his identity in Western society; so, he began to write and define and label. He first wrote under a pseudonym, covering naming conventions for sexual orientations, because up until this point (and for at least seventy years after), there were no "definitive" words that referenced gay men as a whole, as most were regional vernacular. Terms like fairie, pansy, dandy, sexual invert, bugger, Mary, Molly, Tommie, all referred to queer men at different times in history, and in different regions of the world. The words Ulrichs chose to use were, "urnings" for gay men and "dionings" for lesbians: both were created from Greek classics, Uranus and Dione respectively. It was in his search for a label, that his colleague, Karl-Maria Kertbeny (1824-1882) coined the term "homosexual" in a letter to Ulrichs in 1868. Kertbeny went on to publish both "homosexual" and "heterosexual" publicly in 1869.

New York City in the 1860s saw a surge of organized, underground drag events, or as they would be known, drag balls. The balls themselves derived in part from a Black American tradition called "the cakewalk." The cakewalk was a "prize walk" dance, originated by people who were enslaved on plantations, where couples (usually two people assigned male at birth, with one dressed presenting female), would dance down an aisle in front of the other guests, and the best couple/dancers would win titles and prizes (think *Soul Train's* stroll). This general summation of cakewalks would go on to be the outline for most of American drag culture. In NYC, these underground events were spread all over the city, but nowhere were they more lively, intersectional, and extravagant than in Harlem. One of the reasons for this was because Harlem was one of the only places that did not harshly enforce segregation. The novelist, social activist, and icon of the Harlem Renaissance, Langston Hughes (1901-1967) wrote in his autobiography, *The Big Sea* (1940) about one of the most infamous of these Harlem balls. In it, he described the patrons of the gathering as "the queerly assorted throng on the dancing floor, males in flowing gowns and feathered headdresses and females in tuxedos and box-back suits." The queer party to which he was referring was the Grand United Order of Odd Fellows' annual ball at Rockland Palace Casino, and this event had been occurring every year since 1867. When it first began it was called the Hamilton Lodge's Masquerade and Civic Ball, but over time it was given nicknames like the "Fairies' Ball" or "Faggots' Ball," and was one of the few places that queer people could come and be themselves for the day without (mostly) any fear of what that could mean for their safety. A work from the Great Depression's Writers Program* entitled, *The Hamilton Lodge Ball* by Abram Hill, is five pages of in-depth details of the ball during the 1930s. Hill described the ball as a place where,

> "Effeminate men, sissies, 'wolves', 'fairies', the third sex, 'ladies of the night', and male prostitutes got together for a grand jamboree of dancing, love making, display… coming to a climax at the awarding of prizes."

He even noted that by 1936, the last year of the event, it was so popular that approximately 8,000 people attended. It also happened to be the first year that a Black contestant, Miss Jean La'Marr, won the ball. The popularity of the Rockland event is what kept it protected: it often drew in well-connected white patrons, and so where many smaller balls were raided by police, this ball was left unbothered for the most part, which led to its continuation for almost seventy years.

*NY state government paid writers for their work, while the Depression had people unemployed.

Best friends Thomas Ernest Boulton (1847-1901) and Frederick William Park (c.1846-1881) did everything together, and that included doing drag, and being arrested together on April 28, 1870. The two had somewhat parallel lives when it came to their gender expression. Both enjoyed dressing in female-presenting clothing from a young age and went against their fathers' wishes in career paths to pursue drag. While in drag, Boulton went by Stella and Park went by Fanny, a name given to him by his brother, who was also gay. Fanny and Stella would not only go out on the town at night, but they would do daytime drag when they felt like it, which drew the attention of the Bow Street police, who already knew Boulton from previous sex-working charges. When the pair was finally arrested, it became a huge sensation, not only because they showed up for their first court appearance the morning after the arrest still in their gowns, but also due to Boulton (Stella)'s being involved with a member of Parliament. Boulton was serious enough about Lord Arthur Clinton (1840-1870) that they had cards printed that referred to themself as "Lady Arthur Clinton." In court, the two said they were only out in public dressed in gowns for a "lark" or just for fun, which was the go-to excuse for transgender people and drag queens/kings when arrested, and this was because a lark implied it was "only this one time." Stella and Fanny were charged with "attempted sodomy," and after almost a year, their trial began; but luckily for them, the prosecution could offer no proof or witnesses to this "crime." They were found not guilty, and only fined for the "moral offense" of appearing in public in female-presenting clothing. After the trial, the duo used their minor fame to tour with theater companies, both working in smaller bits until each of them passed away.

❧ ❧ ❧ ❧

During the United States' history there have been countless wars, many of which are rarely taught in schools, one being the Great Sioux War of 1876. The cause of the war is none too shocking—the US government wanted to steal more of the Indigenous populations' land and decimate their cultures—but what is interesting about this conflict is one of the warriors who fought at the Battle of the Rosebud. It was said that due to this battle, she got her name, Osh-Tisch (translated to "Finds Them and Kills Them"). A member of the Crow Nation, Osh-Tisch earned her name when she rescued a fellow warrior during the battle, all while taking out enemies. She was a brave and fierce opponent, a medicine woman, artisan, and she was also a boté (or baté) person, which means "not man, not woman." Boté people were typically assigned male at birth and expressed their gender/social role in a female-associated way; they were also the focus of the US government and missionaries when it came to "assimilation." Around the 1890s, government agents began to come into the Crow Nation tribal lands, and force boté people to cut their hair and dress in the clothing that tied to the sex they were assigned at birth. This was something that the leaders of the Crow Nation could not stand, and they fought to expel the agents from Crow territory, which did work for some time, but not forever, and slowly the presence of boté people declined over time.

❧ ❧ ☙ ☙

To avoid police raids, some LGBTQIA+ gatherings would change the locations at which they were held. At times this would work, but in the case of the Temperance Hall ball in Manchester, England, it did not. On September 24,1880, the morning of the event, the police were given a tip that people of "immoral" behavior were going to be throwing a ball. The queer people had rented the hall under a false story and name, so the police were quick to believe the information, and went to stake out the location. Around 9 p.m. people started to arrive, and as noted in the London *Evening Standard* three days later, they were mostly,

"Young men, who in most instances brought portmanteaus (suitcases) or tin boxes with them. A considerable number were in female attire and among the costumes were several low-bodied dresses. In all 47 persons entered the building, and of these 22 were dressed as women."

Once inside the hall, however, the police could not observe what was happening, and that was because, as was incredibly common among LGBTQIA+ people and our spaces, the queer patrons had drawn every blind, and any window without one had paper stuck over it, so that no one could see through. That is, all but one window

Women Who Donned Men's Garb Released

Tell Judge That They Were Out for New Year Lark.

Mrs. Louise Favorman and Mrs. Celia Maiman, who were arrested in Jackson street New Year's Eve for masquerading in male attire appeared before Police Judge Crist yesterday. The cases were dismissed after it had been explained to the court that the women merely had been out for a lark.

Example of "lark" being used to evade charges. San Francisco, 1914.

near the roof, which was cracked to allow ventilation, but also allowed the police to witness the ball. It was reported that the cops watched the ball for hours and after the unnecessary long "observation," they approached the entry door and, according to the London *Evening Standard*,

> "Knocked gently at the door, but received no answer. He knocked in all seven times, and then some person inside said—'Who's there?' The officer had learned that the password adopted among the company was 'Sister,' and, imitating a female's voice, he gave the word. The door was at once opened, and the police rushed into the building."

Though the forty-seven people at the ball put up a fight, they were all arrested and charged with "soliciting and inciting each other to commit improper actions." They were all held at the town hall and because the raid was reported in the newspaper, along with the names and addresses of those charged (as was common through the beginning of the twentieth century), crowds began to show up to see the men in drag. After all the sensation, and reputation destruction, the men were only punished legally with two sureties of £25 each (roughly £2,200, or $3,000 USD today), and 12 months of no other offenses.

❧ ❧ ❧ ❧

Since LGBTQIA+ meeting locations were constantly being raided, a need for private, permanent spaces became apparent, and in London around 1880, the solution for well-off gay men was the Hundred Guineas Club. The club was luxurious and discreet. For the price given in the name, which would equate to about £6,900 or $9,600 USD today, members were given a space to engage in queer love,

drink, dance, and drag shows. The patrons ranged from the upper echelons of society, like dukes and princes to the layman and infantry soldiers, and many took on drag names while in the club. One of the famous names that was rumored to be a member was Prince Albert Victor (1864-1892), the grandson of Queen Victoria, and the second-in-line to the throne of the United Kingdom. He was said to go by the drag name Victoria, for his grandmother, and partook in numerous affairs with men and women in his short life, even being a part of a queer scandal three years before his death, known as the Cleveland Street Scandal (to be discussed in a bit).

In 1886, after almost seven years of assisting the Bureau of American Ethnology (BAE) in its research and understanding of Zuni people, We'Wha (1849-1896), a lhamana person, finally traveled to Washington DC and became the talk of the town. Assigned male at birth, they became an orphan at four years old, after their parents died from smallpox brought by American colonizers. After this, they moved with their brother to their paternal aunt's home to be raised. While We'Wha was growing up, Zuni people had not yet been fully forced to assimilate in American society, which allowed them to practice their culture and customs freely, including the celebration of lhamana people. Though some lhamana people started socially identifying this way as young as four, We'Wha began taking part in the traditions and customs around age twelve, and once they were recognized as lhamana, their education and practices shifted from male-centered to female-centered. It was in these tasks that We'Wha excelled, from weaving to pottery making, and became one of the most well-respected people in their community. In 1879, when Matilda Coxe Stevenson (1849-1915), the first female ethnologist and researcher from BAE, arrived in the Zuni Nation (modern day New Mexico) to study and document the people, it was We'Wha with whom she bonded. Stevenson remarked not only on the talent that We'Wha demonstrated, but also on their vast intelligence and ability to learn multiple languages, including English, so quickly. After multiple visits and correspondences, in 1886, We'Wha stayed with Stevenson in DC, and took part in numerous events and educational lectures. They were in a show at the National Theater, demonstrated traditional Zuni weaving techniques at the Smithsonian, and even met President Grover Cleveland. In most of the newspapers of the time, they are viewed or referred to as a ciswoman, and We'Wha never cared to correct this misconception. Though Stevenson clearly cared for her friend, and understood that they were something beyond the binary, she still tried labeling We'Wha, but did so in a way attempting to honor their identity outside of their assigned sex. In her professional work and personal diaries, she goes from referring to We'Wha by masculine pronouns at their first meeting to feminine pronouns later, even noting after We'Wha's death that,

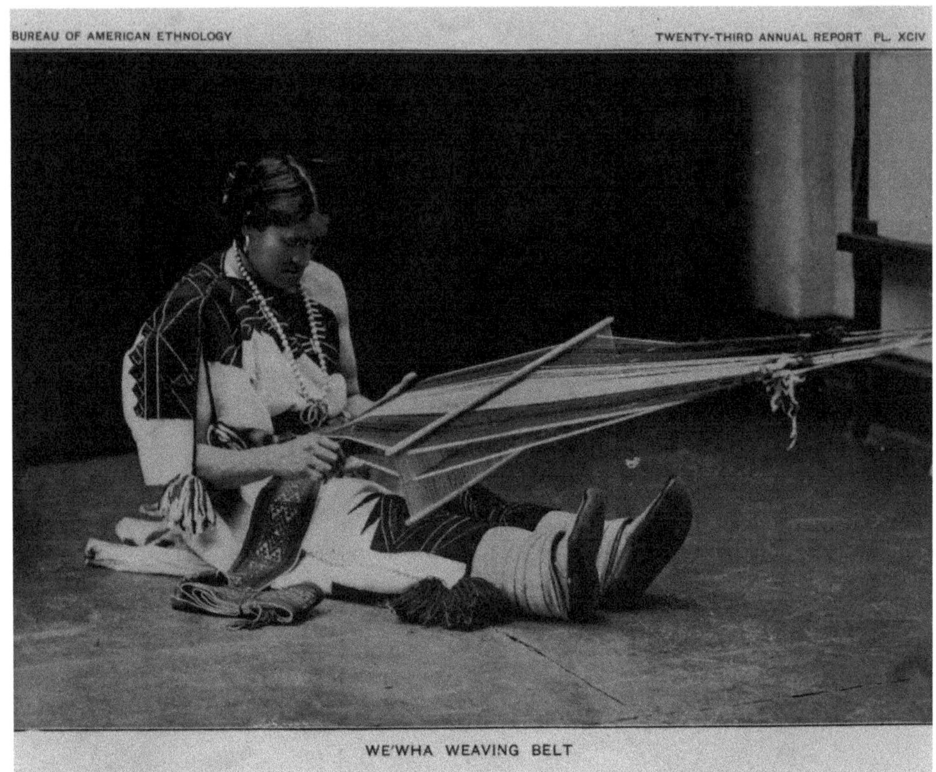

WE'WHA WEAVING BELT

> "As the writer could never think of her faithful and devoted friend in any other light, she will continue to use the feminine gender when referring to We'wha."

❧ ❧ ❧ ❧

Loving queer relationships have consistently been rewritten to appear like platonic friendships, to the point that by 1887 there was a distinct term for lesbian relationships that history would like to pretend were just "close friendships," and that was, "Boston marriages." When writers and historians saw two people of the same gender identity living together, sharing a bed, writing love letters, and committed to each other to the point of being buried together, they claimed that those people were just good friends, and that people were "more affectionate" at the time. The saying "Boston marriage" is said to derive from two things: the romantic relationships that were common among the students at all-female colleges in New England, and *The Bostonians* (1886) by Henry James, a novel which centered around the relationship of two women who were suffragists. Other terms had existed as well, such as "romantic friendships," and "Wellesley marriage," the former usually referring to gay male relationships and the latter to lesbian relationships and deriving from their commonplace at Wellesley College in Massachusetts. All these terms were meant to diminish and erase real, visible relationships that were occurring and had occurred throughout time. Examples of queer relationships that have been straight-washed are everywhere, even in the most visible parts of history, like those of Abraham Lincoln (1809-1865). The 16th president had known relationships with both Joshua Fry Speed (1814-1882), whom he shared a bed with for over four years, and David Derickson, who was his bodyguard. In a letter from a politician's wife, it was noted that Derickson was so "devoted to the president, drives with him, and when Mrs. L. is not home, sleeps with him." Another erased relationship is that of Katherine Lee Bates (1859-1929), the author of *America the Beautiful*, and her partner Katharine Coman, both of whom were professors at

Wellesley College. You will be hard pressed to find a historical reference where it states, so-and-so is "most likely" straight, or "potentially, but there is no hard evidence" of their heterosexual identity, and that is because it is the "assumed" descriptor. Queer is the thing that is treated as if it must be proved consistently, over-and-over, or it does not exist; but, as seen throughout history, LGBTQIA+ people are not literal fairies who need to be believed in or given attention to exist (though it would be nice, and we are magical).

The person credited with founding the profession of social work and co-founder of the American Civil Liberties Union (ACLU), happens to be a lesbian from Chicago named Jane Addams (1860-1935). In her life she accomplished more things than most people could even dream. One of the largest and most important to her was the creation of the Hull House in 1889 with her then-partner (both business and romantic), Ellen Starr (1859-1940). The Hull House was a settlement house, which was a concept that came from a reformist movement of social change beginning around 1884. Settlement houses were built in lower income communities and were meant to provide education, childcare, healthcare, and other resources for local residents. During the movement, Addams' house became the standard to which all others were compared, and by 1911 the complex had grown from one building to thirteen, and essentially operated as a microcosm for the residents. The complex included a public kitchen, art gallery, apartments, library, gym, night classes for adults, employment assistance, and countless other social services. In the 1890s Addams' relationship with Starr ended, and she met Mary Rozet Smith (1868-1934), who would become her new business and romantic partner for the rest of their lives. With Smith's support, Addams was able to continue to actively pursue her passion for social change, particularly addressing financial class disparity and global pacifism. In fact, she won a Nobel Peace Prize for the latter passion in 1931, making her the first American female to win the award. Addams' legacy endures today, from helping improve workers' compensation to aiding in the creation of the Juvenile Protective Association, which was meant to protect children from neglect and abuse. She was also a vocal advocate for other marginalized groups. This included being one of the founding members of the NAACP. Today, two of the Hull House buildings remain as National Landmarks, to pay homage to this queer icon.

☙ ☙ ❧ ❧

In the late nineteenth century, Sándor Vay (1859-1918) had become one of Hungary's most popular journalists, but he is most remembered for his marriage to his second wife, which led to his arrest and subsequent trial. Vay was assigned female at birth but happened to be raised with more masculine-leaning activities, which he took to immediately and preferred. By the age of twenty-one, he

was exclusively presenting male both in private and public, and worked as a freelance writer for some of the most prestigious newspapers in Hungary. With Vay's mild fame, and moderate family wealth, came a bit of drinking, and some duels. He had a reputation around town for being somewhat of a troublemaker at the local night clubs, and that bad boy persona garnered him a few love interests. He was with his first wife for four years before he met and fell in love with Mari Engelhardt, who would become his next wife. Engelhardt's family disapproved of the relationship and so the couple eloped in 1889, much to the chagrin of Engelhardt's parents. After the wedding, Vay borrowed some money from his new father-in-law under the guise of an investment, but really it was to pay some debts. His new father-in-law pressed fraud charges, and Vay was arrested and thrown in jail. While he was in prison a physical exam was performed, and a case was brought forward against him based on his sex assigned at birth. Multiple witnesses were brought in, some of whom had high social standing in Budapest. All the witnesses came to the defense of Vay, and in the end it was determined that he was an "invert," which was the term used for queer people at the time, and thus he could not "control" the way he presented and acted, so he was acquitted on all charges. Not only were all the charges dropped, but he was also left to be allowed to present the way he identified and not the way he was assigned at birth.

☙ ☙ ❧ ❧

What started as a mundane post office investigation into a messenger with extra cash in 1889 led to one of the most notorious gay scandals and potential government cover-ups in England's history. The Cleveland Street Scandal all started at the General Post Office (GPO), where the set up was the post office would monitor the messengers as they would come and go, and one of the rules was

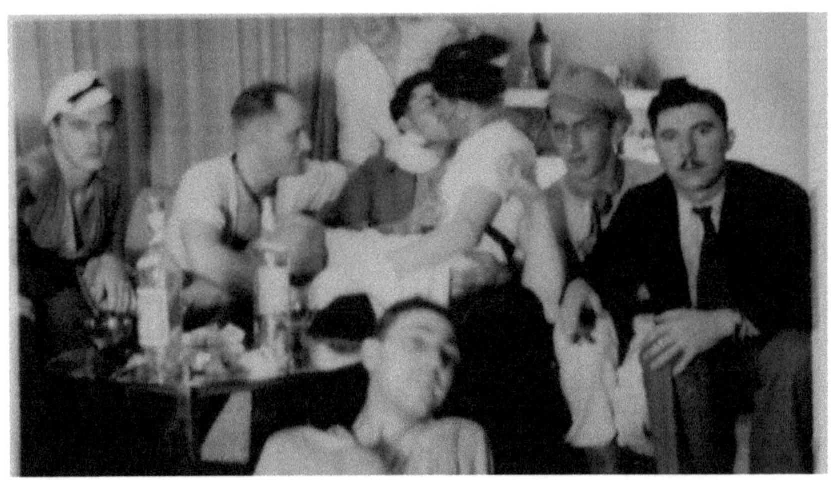

that the messengers could not carry their own money during work, so as to not mix their own cash with customers'. When one boy had almost three weeks' worth of pay on him, he was immediately questioned, and quickly told the investigators that he was a "rent boy," a term for a sex worker at the time, and that he had been presented the opportunity at the post office. He was recruited by a co-worker named Henry Newlove, who had brought several messengers to work at 19 Cleveland Street. The house on Cleveland Street was a brothel, aimed specifically at a clientele of rich, gay men. Through the gay telephone chain, the warning went out, and the house was mostly cleared out when it was finally raided, but what the investigators and newspapers did get was a list of high-ranking aristocrats who were frequent visitors to the Cleveland Street brothel. It is believed that because the connections went so high (Prince Albert Victor, mentioned prior), the scandal was not pursued, and the few punishments that were given out were lighter than usual. One of the other names involved was Henry FitzRoy, Earl of Euston, who, even though he was a known gay man, decided to sue one of the newspapers for libel for publishing that he was involved in the brothel. It was in the libel trial that followed that most of the details of the scandal came out, particularly from a sex worker named John Saul (1857-1904). Saul was brought in for the newspaper's defense to testify to Lord Euston's queer love affairs, and he certainly told all. His testimony was said to be so explicit that it "reduced the court to shocked silence." He proudly talked about being a sex worker, referring to himself as a professional Mary-Ann and rent boy during the trial, and explaining how he had lived at the brothel for the last two years, working there full time. Even after all this testimony, and an on-the-record confession to breaking the law, Saul was never arrested or bothered by the police, which has led to some speculation that he may have had other well-connected clients. There is also a book that is rumored to be his erotic autobiography, *The Sins of the Cities of the Plain* (1881), that was published prior to his time at Cleveland Street (more on this book later).

Thanks to a transman named Dr. Alan L. Hart (1890-1962), the death toll for tuberculosis (TB) between the 1920s and the 1940s (when antibiotics were finally developed) was cut by 80%. Hart had degrees from University of Oregon, University of Pennsylvania, and Yale (to name a few) and devoted much of his career to the study and treatment of tuberculosis, with a focus in helping lower income patients. He was able to develop a screening for TB using Roentgen rays (early x-rays) that caught the illness early enough to treat, and this saved thousands of lives. In his personal life, Hart was also a pioneer. He presented male from early childhood, and his family was accepting of it, never forcing him to wear female-associated clothing. It was not until he was twelve and attended a private school that he was made to wear dresses. While in school he was known for having "boyish" mannerisms, flirtations with a few of his female classmates, and excelling in his courses. By 1917, he had graduated and become a doctor, and had started presenting male publicly. He was ready to begin his authentic life, and for him, that included medical interventions. After he approached a doctor at the University of Oregon, Hart became one of the first men to receive a hysterectomy in the world. From there he legally changed his name in court, which allowed for his medical degrees to change from his birth name to his real name, and for his works to be recognized as such. Dr. Hart was a visible ancestor, who not only worked hard to show that transgender existence is real and valid, but that we can and do lead successful lives.

One of queer Hollywood's biggest allies was born in 1893, and her name was Dorothy Parker (1893-1967). She was once quoted as saying, "heterosexuality is not normal, it's just common," and it was not just with her words that she showed her partnership to marginalized people. Being something more than a performative ally was vital to her and when she passed away, she left her entire estate (including licensing of her works) to Martin Luther King Jr. and in turn, the NAACP. Parker was a screenwriter, poet, and critic, who held strong beliefs and was not shy about telling people, which led to her being blacklisted in Hollywood during the Hays Code and

Communist scares. Though she was not queer-identifying herself, she was a vocal supporter of the community, and said that she preferred the company of gay people to straight-identifying people. Her ex-husband (twice), friend, and writing partner, Alan Campbell was a bisexual man, with whom Parker co-wrote *A Star is Born* (1937, later remade with Lady Gaga in 2018). She also threw lavish, exclusive parties where a vast majority of the guests were queer, and the password to get in was along the lines of, "I'm a friend of Dorothy," which is one of two theories for the origins of the gay euphemism (which is "friend of Dorothy"), the other being Dorothy from *Wizard of Oz*. The term "friend of Dorothy" was, and is, used as a coded way to say that someone is gay without the people in the surrounding area being able to know. The success of this coded phrase remaining a secret from the cis/het world can be seen in the US Navy's mid-1980s investigation into what they believed was an underground network of gay men, run by a woman named Dorothy. The background on this is that a sailor named Mel Dahl, who was discharged for being gay in 1984, had sued the Navy and during the suit mentioned that there were numerous gay men at the Naval Station Great Lakes base. The Navy took this information and then proceeded to send undercover investigators to local gay hangouts, where they overheard men saying, "he's a friend of Dorothy." Not being aware of the context within the community, they believed that there was a literal woman named Dorothy, with whom all these gay men were friends, and that she controlled the secret queer network. To make matters worse for the government (besides the fact that this happened embarrassingly recently), when they brought in sailors to interrogate about this presumed gay overlord, the sailors they caught were all too young to know the reference and correct the mistake, which only seemed to further push the Navy's belief that it was all real. It is said that the government wasted tens of thousands of dollars on this fruitless (pun intended) investigation.

☙ ☙ ❧ ❧

The first-ever transgender activism group is believed to have been started in 1895 by transfeminine sex workers in New York City. The group was called Cercle Hermaphroditos and they met at Paresis Hall, located at 392 Bowery, a place known for being a LGBTQIA+ meeting spot and brothel. The group set out with transwomen and their safety in mind, looking for "extreme types—such as like to doll themselves up in feminine finery," and their mission was to "unite for defense." Almost all of what is known about this group comes from the presumed founder, Jennie June (1874- *after* 1922). In June's own words, she felt as though she was, "doomed to be a girl who must pass her earthly existence in a male body." Her words remain today in the form of two autobiographies that are both raw and heartfelt, and the world has these books thanks to June's cunning. Beginning in 1873 you could not use the USPS to mail material deemed "obscene, lewd or lascivious," but the USPS was how you needed to sell and mail books in the early twentieth century. To the US government, queer-themed works were obscene, with one exception, if the book was of a medical reference. Wanting to get her book published and to be able to send it out, June got a job at *Medico-legal Journal* under the name Earl Lind, changed the name on her manuscript to Ralph Werther, and then got her boss to agree to write the introduction and order 1,000 copies. And so, in 1918, *Autobiography of an Androgyne* was published for the first time, and gave the world one transwoman's experience, from joyous to sometimes painfully uncomfortable, but all of it real for her.

As the Western world of male thinkers was attempting to categorize and name the spectrum of sexualities, Emma Trosse (1863-1949), a German teacher and writer, decided to skirt convention and the law banning women from lecture halls, and make her voice heard. Trosse began writing on LGBTQIA+ issues in 1895, when she published *Der Konträrsexualismus in Bezug auf Ehe und Frauenfrage* (*Contrary-Sexuality in Relation to Marriage and the Women Question*). This work would be one of the first educational pieces by a woman on lesbianism and argued that LGBTQIA+ people deserved rights and recognition based on the fact that the spectrum of sexuality was naturally occurring and valid. She was also one of the first people to focus particularly on "asensuality," or asexuality as it is known now, and even wrote in her work that the

"Author has the courage to admit to this category." This admission makes Trosse one of the first people to publicly identify as asexual, a sexuality that accounts for approximately one percent of the population or 78,000,000 people.

☙ ☙ ❧ ❧

During Oscar Wilde's (1854-1900) life his works were celebrated, and over a century after his death, his writings are still read in schools and performed on stages. Wilde was known for adding his signature wit into his writings, as well as nods to the more flamboyant aspects of the world, and it was the latter part that

would be his downfall. Though Wilde was a married father of two, it was widely known that he saw rent boys as well as having a few serious male relationships. The most pivotal began in 1891 with Lord Alfred Douglas (1870-1945), the man over whom Wilde would effectively lose his career. Douglas' father was the Marquess of Queensberry (1844-1900), a man who is credited with inventing the rules for modern boxing and who had no tolerance for anything even remotely queer. When the Marquess found out about the relationship between his son and Wilde, he threatened Wilde and told him to never see his son again, to which Wilde balked. The feud escalated with the Marquess planning to embarrass Wilde by throwing rotting vegetables at a stage during the performance of one of his plays (yes, really), but Wilde found out beforehand and had the Marquess banned from the theater. The Marquess' next blow was leaving a "calling card" at Wilde's club, a calling card was essentially an "expose her" video/post of the day. The calling card was a simple sentence and it said, "For Oscar Wilde posing Somdomite." The Marquess of Queensberry had publicly called Wilde a sodomite (although his spelling was off, guess the Marquess should leave the writing to Wilde), and since being gay was a crime, Wilde decided to sue for libel. The issue with suing for libel, is that libel means someone wrote something that was not true, and as we know, this accusation was in fact the truth. The verdict of this trial was the Marquess' acquittal, and the issuing of a warrant for Wilde's arrest for sodomy and gross indecency, which led to several of his friends fleeing England for fear that they would be next. During his trial in 1895, Wilde did not seem to attempt to hide who he was, and when he was questioned about a line that Douglas had written to him which referenced a "love that dare not speak its name," Wilde did not hold back on its meaning. In an eloquent, almost poetic manner, Wilde listed a history of gay lovers, and the natural occurrence of his love, saying,

> "It is in this century misunderstood, so much misunderstood that it may be described as 'the love that dare not speak its name', and on that account of it I am placed where I am now. It is beautiful, it is fine, it is the noblest form of affection. There is nothing unnatural about it."

This trial also did not end in Wilde's favor, and he was sentenced to two years in prison. While in prison his health declined and it directly contributed to his death, but Wilde created one last work, *De Profundis*, which was written as a letter to Douglas and outlined the lead up to his imprisonment and life in prison.

❧ ❧ ❧ ❧

The original, self-proclaimed "queen of drag" was not RuPaul, but a formerly enslaved queen named William Dorsey Swann (c.1858-*after* 1900), and he ran the drag scene in Washington DC during the 1880s-90s. Swann threw the most well-known balls of the time, with secret invites going out through local gay spots, like the

Real photo postcard from the 1902 cakewalk tour of Charles Gregory (left) and Brown (right), who is more than likely Willam Dorsey Swann.

YMCA, and catering to Black and white patrons alike. The balls were extravagant, featuring dancing, drag, drinking, and cakewalk (the Black American prize walk tradition developed by people who were enslaved). It was the popularity of the events that led to Swann's iconic reputation, several arrests, and widespread newspaper coverage. When he was arrested in 1888, the headline of the report in *The National Republican* was, "'The Queen' Raided. Unexpected Interruption to Her Banquet and Ball," and it discussed the raid and how the guests were dressed in beautiful gowns made of satin and silk. Swann managed to not be arrested again until the morning of New Year's Day 1896. Unlike his other arrests, where he was given fines and minimal jail sentences, if any, the charge in this situation was "running a disorderly house," which was used typically for houses that sex workers worked from or places that LGBTQIA+ people congregated, and it carried a stiffer punishment. Three days after his arrest he was sentenced to ten months in prison, but this was not going to silence him, and just three months into his sentence, Swann decided to file a petition to request a pardon from President Cleveland. Though the pardon was denied, it makes Swann the first person to take legal recourse to defend LGBTQIA+ people's right to assemble. Another incredible note about Swann is the potential that he is also part of the international touring cakewalk duo Charles Gregory and Brown (Swann). The pair, with Swann (Brown) in drag, traveled through France on a tour performing the cakewalk, and garnered mild fame. Another queer fact about the duo is that in 1903 the Lumière Brothers, pioneers in film, recorded a fifty-seven-second video of the pair dancing, which makes Swann the first ever drag queen to be recorded on film, and makes duo one of the first queer presenting couples to appear on film.

☙ ☙ ❧ ❧

Named after the final battle of the Sacred Band of Thebes, the Order of Chaeronea was a secret society for gay men (and a handful of lesbians) formed in 1897. The Order was created by George Cecil Ives (1867-1950) to covertly connect queer people and start to align on a community level to enact change. Ives wanted to push "the Cause," which was the "liberation" of queer people to be able to love freely in the world, and he was in good company in England. He was friends with Oscar Wilde and was even said to have had an affair with Lord Alfred Douglas, both of whom are thought to have been on the 300+ member list of the Order, though the list no longer survives. Ives' devotion to advancing queer people did not end with the Order of Chaeronea. In 1914 he helped form the British Society for the Study of Sex Psychology (BSSSP), which addressed topics from sexuality to birth control to sex work.

☙ ☙ ❧ ❧

The first woman to own a printing company in Detroit, MI is also the woman given the nickname of "oldest surviving lesbian." Her name was Ruth Ellis and her life spanned three centuries, beginning in 1899 and lasting until 2000. She was the first generation of her family to be born outside of slavery, and her father became the first Black postal carrier in Illinois. Ellis knew who she was from an early age and was fortunate enough to have a family that did not try and change or suppress her identity. There was one time when she had a girlfriend over at her family house and her father did not make the situation seem "unnatural," she said. "We made a little too much noise. The only thing my father ever said to me was, 'Next time you girls make that much noise, I will put you both out.'" Ellis was aware of how fortunate she was, and when she had a home of her own, she opened it to LGBTQIA+ kids who were without homes or families of their own. The home of Ellis and her partner, Ceciline "Babe" Franklin (c.1909-1975), was known in Detroit as "The Gay Spot," and she made continuous effort over her entire life to uplift the underserved queer kids of her community, particularly the queer kids of color. Ellis' impact was so important and widespread throughout Detroit that there is a community center in Highland Park named after her (the Ruth Ellis Center), whose mission it is to continue Ellis' legacy and serve the LGBTQIA+ youth of the area.

Chapter Three: Yaass, Turning the Century (1900-1945)

As the century turned to 1900, queer people were turning the party and had established several LGBTQIA+ annual events and safe havens across Europe, all meant for dancing, fun, and freedom. In Spain, the sociedades de baile (ball societies) had established several clubs in Madrid and Barcelona that varied in size and extravagance. Some of the spaces were halls rented for the night, while others were giant, lavish theaters used for daily drag balls. France was known for its queer literary salons, where people would meet with the intention of sharing knowledge with one another. In Paris, specifically at Magic City Amusement Park located at 188 rue de l'Université, was a massive drag ball held annually that attracted thousands of people in its later years. Reminders of these balls are left from famed photographer Brassaï (1899-1994), who documented nightlife in Paris, including queer lives. Berlin was the pinnacle of turn-of-the-century European queer nightlife, with their Urningsballs or Tuntenballs (essentially gay or drag balls) that were so popular that they were considered tourist attractions. Gay Berlin, as it was coined, is usually considered the original capital of gay culture in Europe, being the home to the first-ever gay publication,

Der Eigene (*The Self-Owning*) which ran from 1896-1932 and having one of the first unofficial LGBTQIA+ "districts." Over the course of the first decade or so of the twentieth century, Berlin had clubs for everyone: lesbians would frequent Mali and Ingel, gay men had Karls-Lounge, transmen and drag kings went to Silhouette, transwomen and drag queens turned up at Mikado, and the crown jewel of it all was the Eldorado Cafe, where anyone and everyone met to dance and party. The Eldorado was the center of gay Berlin, drawing in famous names like Marlene Dietrich and Erika and Klaus Mann. It was like this up until 1932 when all places that held "amusements with dancing of a homosexual nature" were given a curfew of 10pm. The next year, Hitler came to power and expanded Paragraph 175 (Germany's anti-queer law) making anything, including perceived gay flirtation, a criminal offense. This would be one of many blows the Nazis would deal to queer culture and history. They even attacked the gay men within their own ranks on the Night of the Long Knives, which was an event that took place over a three-day span in the summer of 1934 when Hitler ordered the execution of anyone who he deemed a threat. It so happened that many of those "threats" were the gay men within the paramilitary branch of the Sturmabteilung (SA). ** The SA was run by an out gay man, and his effective control over this army (that also happened to include a large number of queer people) became the largest looming threat to Hitler's continued power.

**A point to make here is that experiencing one type of oppression does not exempt a person from being an oppressor, and we must actively be working on educating ourselves.

❧ ❧ ☙ ☙

El baile de los cuarenta y uno or The Dance of the Forty-one refers to a police raid on a drag ball in Mexico City in 1901 that is so infamous the number "41" became synonymous with queer life. At this point in Mexican history, gay sexual relationships were not illegal, but breaking the hetero/cisnormative rules was considered a disruption of society, and this would be the burden the drag queens and transwomen of the event would bear. The ball held on the "street of La Paz" actually had forty-two attendees, but the last one was Ignacio de la Torre y Mier, who was married to Amada Diaz, which made him the son-in-law of Mexican President, Porfirio Díaz. This connection allowed his name and arrest to be expunged. In Amada Diaz' journal she wrote of her suspicions being confirmed about her husband's true desires, when her father told her of the arrests at the ball. The raid that occurred was not part of a long sting, but rather was based on a tip that an event without a permit was going to happen. When the police entered the premises, all forty-two people who were there were arrested, and nineteen of them were dressed in female presenting attire. By the next day, the number processed was forty-one, with de la Torre's name being erased at the request of Porfirio Díaz. The prevalence of wealth, sexism, and the concept that being or acting female was equivalent to weakness, and thus bad, led the sentencing of the forty-one attendees to be skewed. The men who were arrested in suits were able to buy their way out of any punishment at all, while their nineteen female-presenting counterparts were sentenced harshly. The punishment started with the nineteen having to sweep the streets of the city in their gowns for public humiliation, and then they were sent to serve in the military, but not as soldiers; they were made to work as maids and serve the soldiers as effective forced house/sex workers. Even though Porfirio Díaz attempted to have all the records wiped that mentioned the ball, newspapers and gossip columns never let it disappear. The papers and broadsheets of the time sensationalized aspects, and exaggerated others, purposefully framing the queer people in a poor light. This all led to the tie between "41" and LGBTQIA+ things to be taken so seriously by the cis/het world that for almost half a century the number forty-one was left out of Mexican army battalion numbers, hospital rooms and even in hotels.

❧ ❧ ☙ ☙

Prior to his death in 1901, Murray Hall (1841-1901) was considered a political mover, heavy-drinker, doting father, and a loving, but rarely faithful husband. For more than twenty-five years he was part of the political machine that was Tammany Hall in New York City and assisted in increasing voter turnout amongst the immigrant population of the area. He was an immigrant himself, having moved to the US in 1870 from Ireland, after his first wife outed his transmale identity as revenge for his infidelity. In New York he thrived though, opening his own employment business, yielding political influence at Tammany Hall, marrying twice, and adopting a daughter, whom he called Minnie. It is believed that only his wives knew about his identity, and Hall was known to avoid doctors. He even went to the lengths of teaching himself medicine so that he never had to see one; that was until the week before his death. It was at that point that he requested the local doctor come to his apartment where he showed him the lesions on his chest. He had breast cancer that was so advanced that the doctor gave him only days to live. Hall knew that the one thing he had tried to avoid his whole life would occur after his death, and that was his identity as a man being denied. He was right. Besides being buried in female-presenting clothing and in an unmarked grave (not with his beloved wife), newspapers around the world plastered their pages with articles misgendering and mocking him. Unlike other transmen of the time who would sometimes use makeup to give themselves facial hair, Hall kept a clean face, and once he died, even though it was never thought about before, that, as well as his voice and height, were scrutinized (which are all things that somehow become invasively important once someone learns about a trans person's identity). As a light to Hall's end, he raised a child who loved him as he was, and when his daughter was pushed to call her father "she," Minnie said boldly, "No, I will never say she."

❧ ❧ ❧ ❧

CHARLES PARKHURST, who followed the occupation of a stawe driver for many years, in California, recently died near Watsonville, and the discovery was made that Charley Parkhurst was a perfectly-formed and fully-developed woman. Friends and associates who had known him for years, at first refused to believe it. The cause of the disguise is unknown.

(Above) Article from *The Phoenix Herald* (Jan. 8,1880) covering the death of Charley Parkhurst, who was a transman.

(Below) Pair of transmen sporting mustaches with the help of makeup, c. 1915

On June 8, 1901, Marcela Gracia Ibeas (c.1867-*after* 1920) and Elisa Sánchez Loriga (c.1867-*after* 1904) were married inside a Spanish church, and their marriage is still officially legal, though the document states "Marcella and Mario." The two women met as students in A Coruña, Spain in the early 1880s, and quickly became inseparable, to the point that Ibeas' parents sent her to Madrid to curb the relationship. Fate had other things in mind, and the pair were working within walking distance of each other when they began their careers as teachers. Their relationship ebbed and flowed over the next decade, with the two living together and then separating, eventually leading to them finding each other again and in 1901, deciding that they wanted to be together forever, legally, with a sped up time frame due to Ibeas being pregnant. Loriga cut her hair, put on a suit, called herself Mario, a presumed distant cousin from London, and asked for Ibeas' hand in marriage. "Mario" met the family and the local priest, was baptized in the Catholic faith on May 26th, 1901, and was married to Ibeas on June 8th. Everything went according to plan until neighbors, who had known the couple prior to the marriage, reported them. Newspapers across Spain ran headlines about the "marriage without a man," and arrest warrants for the women were issued. They fled to Portugal where they tried to live as a couple, but that was short-lived as well; since their faces were in the newspapers, they could not escape the threat of extradition. So again, in 1902 they fled, this time to Buenos

Aires, Argentina where they hoped to outrun the impending prison sentences. Little is known about what happened to the pair after this. It is believed that Ibeas married a wealthy man but refused to consummate the marriage which led to her exposure once again. Their love lives on in the form of numerous works from the 1902 book, *La sed de Amar* by Felipe Trigo to Netflix's 2019, *Elisa & Marcela*.

One of the first organized police stings directed at the LGBTQIA+ community in the United States happened at the Ariston Bathhouse in New York City in 1903. Historically, bathhouses have been known to be meeting places for the queer community. In Florence, Italy beginning in 1492 court documents show there was almost a vendetta against the "vice of sodomy" and the places that housed the act, such as taverns, brothels, and bathhouses. In the same year Queen Isabella I of Spain closed all the bathhouses to curb gay sexual encounters. This understanding that queer, mainly gay, men met at bathhouses has been used by governing bodies to entrap and attack the community for centuries, and the Ariston Bathhouse was no different. For weeks leading up to the raid, the police had been watching the business, and sending in undercover officers to document the patrons and what they were doing. When they finally raided the building at 1:45 a.m. on February 21, 1903, they had the exits blocked so that all seventy-eight men inside had no chance to escape. Of the seventy-eight taken in that night, only thirty-four had charges brought against them, and those resulted from the prior weeks of police surveillance. The court cases that followed were explicit, and showed the severe lack of knowledge around gay topics, including sex. In one of the cases, the defense argued that it was physically impossible for two men to have sex standing up, as the officer had claimed, and with two doctors battling on the possibility of this, the defendant was granted a mistrial. There were seven other men who were not as fortunate and were sentenced to multiple years in prison for the crime of simply being gay. The Ariston would be the first of hundreds of similarly planned raids on queer meeting places in NYC, many of them due to the New York Society for the Suppression of Vice (NYSSV). The NYSSV was like the Society for the Reformation of Manners in that it was religiously morality-based, with a focus on suppression of all things deemed "wrong," and a drive for white, cis/het conformity. They also worked in tandem, were financially supported, and legally backed by the NY government. To show exactly what the NYSSV's thoughts were on queer life, particularly in reference to religion, its founder Anthony Comstock once commented in 1900 about the Black Rabbit, a gay club he raided,

> "'Sodom and Gomorrah' would blush for shame at hearing to what depths of vice its habitués had descended."

The first Black Rhodes Scholar (international scholarship to attend Oxford University) was honored in 1907. His name was Alain LeRoy Locke (1885-1954), and he happens to be a gay Harlem Renaissance writing icon. To fully understand this feat, the next time a Black person would be selected for the honor would not happen until 1963. Locke was a pioneer this way; he graduated Harvard in 1907, where he was the first Black person to win the Bowdoin prize, which is one of the school's most prestigious prizes. Though he was highly respected, he was not exempt from racism, and upon arriving at Oxford he was denied entry into several colleges, and racist, white fellow Rhodes Scholars refused to live with him. After pushing, he was able to receive his education at Oxford, and moved on to University of Berlin. He went back to the United States in 1912 and attended Howard University (a Historically Black College). At Howard he found not only a place to continue his doctorate, but also a place to begin his career in education and writing. In 1925, Locke was fired from Howard due to his fighting for equal pay for the Black staff members. It was during this time that he worked with a few other Black activists and published *The New Negro: An Interpretation* (1925), which has come to be considered one of the most important Black American literary works. Locke used his background in philosophy to build on the emerging fight for equality, focusing on the idea of no longer staying complacent and creating social and political change, through ideas that utilized the arts, and focused on political activism, and self-expression. When Howard University hired its first Black president in 1926, Locke was immediately reinstated, and he continued to teach and inspire students there until he retired in 1953.

When *Aus eines Mannes Mädchenjahren* (*Memoirs of a Man's Maiden Years*) came out in 1907, it was published under the pseudonym N.O. Body. The book was part fiction, part autobiography and was co-written by Magnus Hirschfeld and Karl M. Baer (1885-1956). The former was a famed sexologist who devoted his life to advocating for LGBTQIA+ and women's rights (more on his work in a few facts), and the latter was the subject of the autobiographical part of the work, being the recipient of one of the first gender-affirming surgeries. Baer always felt unlike the women whom he spent time with during his activism work, and with the emerging study of sexology, he found doctors who supported his understanding of himself. Hirschfeld advocated for Baer, and Baer in turn helped Hirschfeld with his studies on transgender people, which culminated in the publishing of *Memoirs of a Man's Maiden Years* and, in 1906, Baer receiving gender-affirming surgery. He was able to have the sex on his birth certificate, as well as his name, legally changed, which was one of the first times this occurred in Europe. From there he lived relatively quietly for the remaining years of his life, besides needing to emigrate to Palestine in 1938, due to the Nazis' taking over Germany. He was married twice and outlived both of his wives. He also held numerous jobs from accountant to social worker, and was a respected member of Jewish society, being buried in the Kiryat-Shaul cemetery in Tel Aviv.

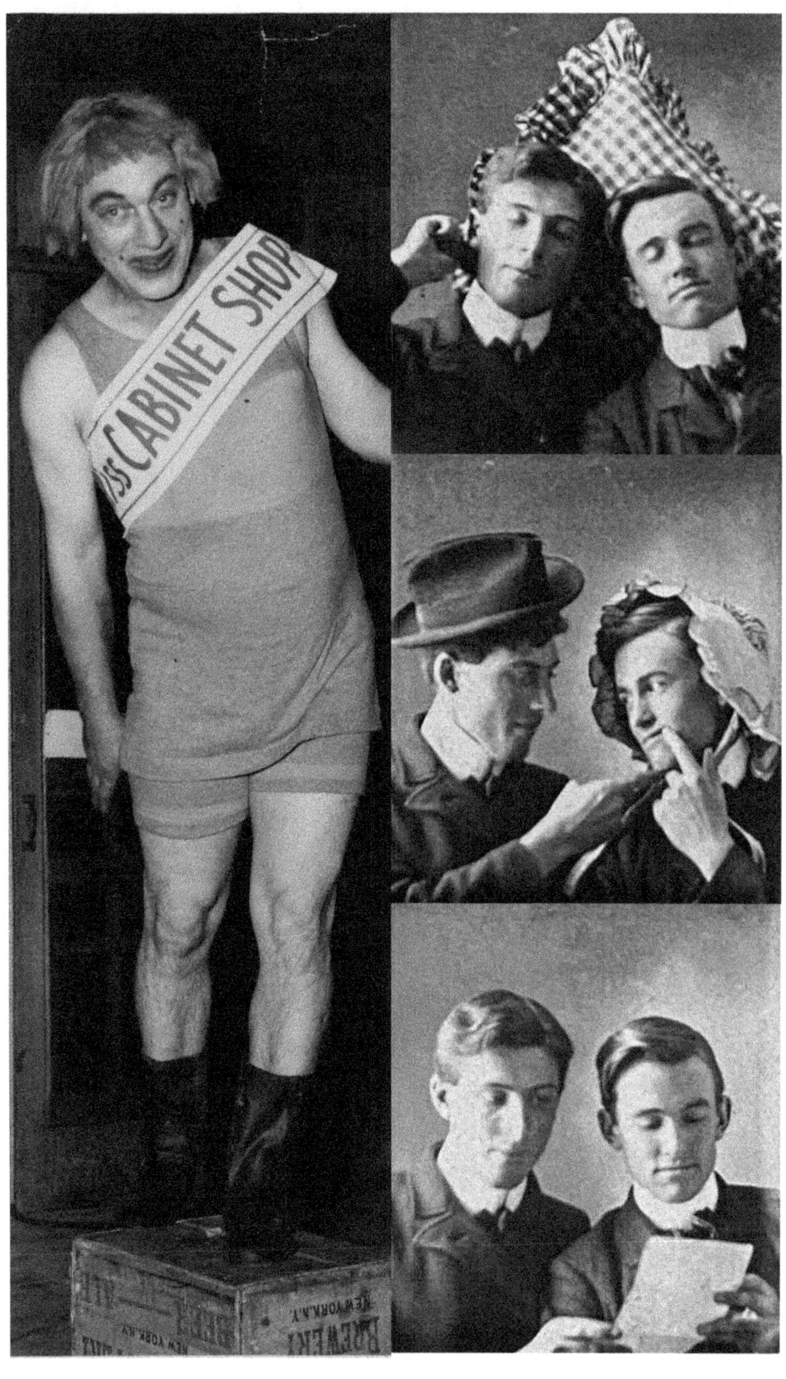
CABINET SHOP

Though they wanted them, LGBTQIA+ people did not need permanent, housed locations to meet, and by the 1910s a few areas in New York City, Central Park in particular, were known gay cruising spots; "cruising" is a queer-coded term that refers to "looking for sex." City Hall Park is one of the earliest known cruising spots, Belvedere Castle was a main pick-up spot in Central Park, as well as the benches near Columbus Circle, while the Ramble was known as "the fruited plain," and they were all the focus of the morality police and undercover cops. Officers would be sent in and would observe the men coming in and out of the park, as well as arresting any man who approached them about sex. This cycle of public areas being queer meccas, and then being invaded by police was extremely common through the twentieth century, both in other places in the US from San Francisco to Philadelphia, to places around the world like the Moorfields of London. Some of the most famous queer icons fell victim to these types of charges, like Harvey Milk (1930-1978) who was arrested in 1947 in Central Park when he was caught without his shirt on, literally, though he would go on to serve in the Korean War and be the first openly gay elected official in California.

❧ ❧ ❧ ❧

Musicians Billy Tipton (1914-1989) and Willmer "Little Axe" Broadnax (c.1916-1996) never met, but the two transmen led extremely similar lives. Both men started presenting male from an early age and each had a passion for music that drove everything they did in life. Tipton was a white man who had a passion for jazz music and performed from band to band until he was finally discovered. In 1957, Tops Records signed him, and he released two albums under the band name, The Billy Tipton Trio. Broadnax was a Black man who had a voice for gospel and spent the 1940s and 50s lending his lead vocals to some of the most celebrated groups, such as the Golden Echoes, the Fairfield Four, and the Spirit of Memphis Quartet. For their later lives, though Tipton was never married, five women called themselves Mrs. Tipton, and he adopted three children. Broadnax was never married, but had several women in his life as well, the final one being the person who killed him. Where their lives converge again is in that when they died their autopsies became the topic of public conversation. Both Broadnax and Tipton kept their transgender identities to themselves, and Tipton had not even shared his identity with his children. Once their identities were published, the public began to analyze everything from their vocal range to height, again all things that were never discussed or acknowledged previously.

❧ ❧ ❧ ❧

When Ralph Kerwineo (1876-1932) left his spouse of almost fifteen years for a younger woman in 1914, the ramification was the world as he knew it. Kerwineo and his then common-law wife, Mamie White had met while at Provident Hospital Nursing School, which was the first Black owned and operated hospital and teaching school in the United States. The pair graduated in 1900 and began traveling the Midwest looking for work, which was scarce for people of color (Kerwineo being Black and Potawatomie-Cherokee). Kerwineo started presenting male privately somewhere around 1903, and White supported him in this. The couple settled in Milwaukee in 1906, and this move to a place of all new people meant Kerwineo could always present as his authentic self. He was well liked in town, and his boss considered him the "best man to ever work" for him. With his popularity came a reputation of being somewhat of a ladies' man, which caused issues with White, and eventually led to the demise of the decades-long relationship. At the end of 1913, Kerwineo met Dorothy Kleinowsky, a twenty-one-year-old, bubbly blonde, and that was it: he left White and married Kleinowsky on March 24, 1914. When White heard of the marriage in May of that year, she sought vengeance and tried outing his trans identity to his work, to little acknowledgement, so she next went to Kleinowsky's mother and then to the district attorney. Kerwineo was arrested, and the trial and scandal began. White claimed that she did not have any romantic feelings for Kerwineo and only took part in the "masquerade" for financial purposes, which would be believable had she not gone *Swimfan* on outing him when she found out he was married. Countless people showed up in his defense, stating how honorable and hardworking he was, which led the judge to suspend all jail sentences and state that Kerwineo was a good, moral man, however, he did also order that Kerwineo wear women's clothing going forward. In reference to the ruling Kerwineo said,

> "I am feminine not again, but still. But my heart and soul are more those of a man than a woman. Now it is hard to reconcile myself that I must go back to my former existence. It seems a joke for me to go back to woman's dress. I think I am masquerading again."

He was able to make money after the trial touring with sideshows, but it did not last long. And as with all things that are authentically us, presenting as himself was not something that Kerwineo could just stop, and he was arrested at least three times in the last decade or so of his life for wearing men's clothing in public.

❧ ❧ ❧ ❧

In 1916, Nobuko Yoshiya (1896-1973) began publishing *Hanamonogatari* (or "Flower Tales") which would, by its final work in 1926, become a collection of fifty-two short stories about unrequited lesbian love. The dedication she wrote for the fully published book says, “The many flowers that bloom/ in the dream of a young girl’s days/ that will never return, these I send to you, my beloveds.” Each one of the fifty-two stories centered around one individual type of flower, either in its plot, title, or imagery, and the collection is considered foundational in the Class S genre of literature and shojo manga (both are Japanese literary forms centered around intense female bonds, for instance Sailor Moon is considered shojo manga). Yoshiya was a pioneer beyond writing (where she is considered one of the most commercially successful Japanese writers): she was also the first woman in Japan to own a car, and lived openly with her partner, Monma Chiyo, for forty-seven years. As a statement of their love, Yoshiya even adopted Chiyo, as was common during the twentieth century for queer people. Adoption allowed for queer people to have access to almost all the benefits of marriage, from medical decisions to sharing a last name, and so it became a loophole for couples since they could not get married. To provide further proof of Yoshiya’s lesbian status, in 1930 she wrote *Danasama muyō* which translates to “Husbands are Unnecessary.” Yoshiya and Chiyo were vocal feminist and dedicated their time to furthering women’s education and equality, even leaving their estate to the city of Kamakura with the intention that it be used to advance and support women's education. The Yoshiya Nobuko Memorial Museum is still open today and is just one part of the legacy that was left by Yoshiya to inspire the world.

❧ ❧ ❧ ❧

Much of the known first-hand history of lesbians during the Harlem Renaissance comes from the stories of Mabel Hampton (1902-1989), as documented by the Lesbian Herstory Archives. Hampton was orphaned, sexually assaulted, and homeless all before the age eight, but she overcame the racism and sexism that she faced and continued to thrive. She held jobs that ranged from a dancer at clubs like the Garden of Joy to domestic worker, and it was in the latter occupation that she met Joan Nestle (b. 1940) and began to document her adventures in the not-so underground world of lesbians during the Harlem Renaissance. Her insight into the intimate details of some of the lesbian parties that occurred during the time, as well as tales of sham marriages, are invaluable bits of everyday life for LGBTQIA+ people in history, particularly queer women of color. In her interviews, Hampton candidly spoke about the love affairs that were going on, as well as the coded, unspoken rules that existed amongst the community to keep it safe and protected during the 1920s and 30s. She lived an exciting life and dedicated an enormous amount of her time to advocating for racial and queer equity, but there was nothing she was prouder of than her thirty-year relationship with the woman she called her wife, Lillian Foster, with whom she lived and loved openly. The core of Hampton is seen in her response to the archaic question of "when did you come out?" Hampton would always quip, "What do you mean? I was never in."

❧ ❧ ❧ ❧

A queer scandal in 1919 related to a Newport, Rhode Island naval base and a YMCA almost derailed Franklin D. Roosevelt's political career and would become one of the most covered pre-Stonewall queer events in "mainstream" media. As is clear, LGBTQIA+ involved events were often downplayed in the media, or simply not covered at all. The media that did cover queer stories were the niche or marginalized newspapers, such as *Variety Magazine* and the *New York Age*. The Newport Scandal as it would be known, was so shocking at the time, that it would be one of the only gay-focused events to be continuously covered in the *New York Times* and other newspapers that were the most widely distributed. The events all started when the United States entered WWI and somewhere between 15,000-20,000 men went to the naval base in Newport for training, a base that was meant to hold 2,000. Sailors were placed in affordable housing near the base, such as the YMCA, which allowed for interaction with the local civilians. In 1919, while in the Naval Station Newport hospital a sailor was invited to attend the gay, drag parties that would happen at night, but this sailor decided to attend and then tattle. The Navy took the information and then enlisted their own sailors to infiltrate these events and partake in the parties, sex, drugs, and all. This two-month sting operation ended with seventeen sailors being arrested and court-martialed on sodomy and scandalous conduct charges. Some were sent to prison and others discharged, with classifications ranging from dishonorable to blue discharge. A blue discharge was an "other than honorable" discharge, used to purge the military of "undesirable" recruits, targeting LGBTQIA+ and BIPOC people specifically. This investigation was a double-edged sword for FDR who was the Assistant Secretary of the Navy at the time. A reverend and an investigative journalist from *The Providence Journal* came forward about the tactics used by FDR and his "vice squad" to obtain evidence, and so a special Senate committee was launched. Over the next two years FDR and the Navy were investigated and finally condemned for their actions, not for invading the private lives of the sailors, but for coercing low-ranking sailors to participate in "unnatural acts" in order to arrest "only a few men of bad character among the thousands." It would be a stain that delayed FDR from running for president, but was then largely forgotten with time, mostly due to the continuous erasure of LGBTQIA+ historical events.

❧ ❧ ❧ ❧

After decades of devoting his life to LGBTQIA+ advocacy, in 1919 German sexologist Magnus Hirschfeld (1868-1935) saw his work culminate in the opening of Institut für Sexualwissenschaft (Institute for Sexology), which was a non-profit research organization located in Berlin. The institute was formed from seeds that began in 1893 after Hirschfeld graduated with his medical degree (1892) and moved to Chicago, IL. While in the Windy City he found a home in the gay-subculture and began to see striking similarities to the queer communities back in Europe, and in this the concept of "universal" queerness emerged; the idea that it is not a choice, and naturally occurring, so much so that there are universally shared traits (it must be noted that his observation of Indigenous people can only be viewed as a white man forcing his narrative onto Indigenous culture). Within three years Hirschfeld had opened a practice serving LGBTQIA+ individuals, and though he was able to advance medical care, many of his patients died by suicide, and this was the turning point from simply doctor to vocal advocate. Hirschfeld founded Wissenschaftlich-humanitäres Komitee (Scientific-Humanitarian Committee) with LGBTQIA+ equity in all aspects of life as its core mission. WhK, as it was known, assisted queer people who were arrested, and argued against Paragraph 175 (Germany's law that criminalized queer relationships) using medical and science-backed evidence. The group was able to gain traction, even being supported by Albert Einstein and Leo Tolstoy, and by 1905 Hirschfeld was able to partner with Helene Stöcker (1869-1943) and her feminist organization, to find both an increase in numbers and allyship in linking women's and queer rights. Hirschfeld became the world's foremost expert on gender studies and treatment, and when his institute finally opened it served more than 20,000 patients a year, from therapy sessions to gender-affirming medical interventions, providing services for free for lower income patients.

The institute was a mecca of queer and intersex studies for doctors and scientists alike, as it was home to the largest collection of LGBTQIA+ archives, from medical research to the original copy of the first pro-gay film, *Anders als die Andern (Different from the Others*, 1919*)*.The reason the existence of this collection is stated in the past tense is that in 1933, after years of harassment and assaults by the Nazi regime, the institute was the target of a final, brutal attack where at least one transwoman, Dörchen Richter, was killed, hundreds of names and addresses of patients were stolen and used by the Nazis, and somewhere between 15,000-20,000 pieces of the first intersex and queer research, photos, and personal journals were publicly burned. Hirschfeld was out of the country hosting lectures at the time, and due to both his gay and Jewish identity, was never able to return home. He lived his remaining years in France, continuing his advocacy of LGBTQIA+ rights, as well as writing about racism in the Western world, specifically using Nazism as an example. He argued that it was not some outlier of Western thought, but just a different degree of the racism that occurs daily, and until the world acknowledges that, white supremacy will continue to be a persistent, looming issue.

❧ ❧ ❧ ❧

In response to cruising, New York passed a legal code in 1923 that was very direct in its intention. It stated that loitering for the "purpose of sodomy" was now a criminal offense, and with this the

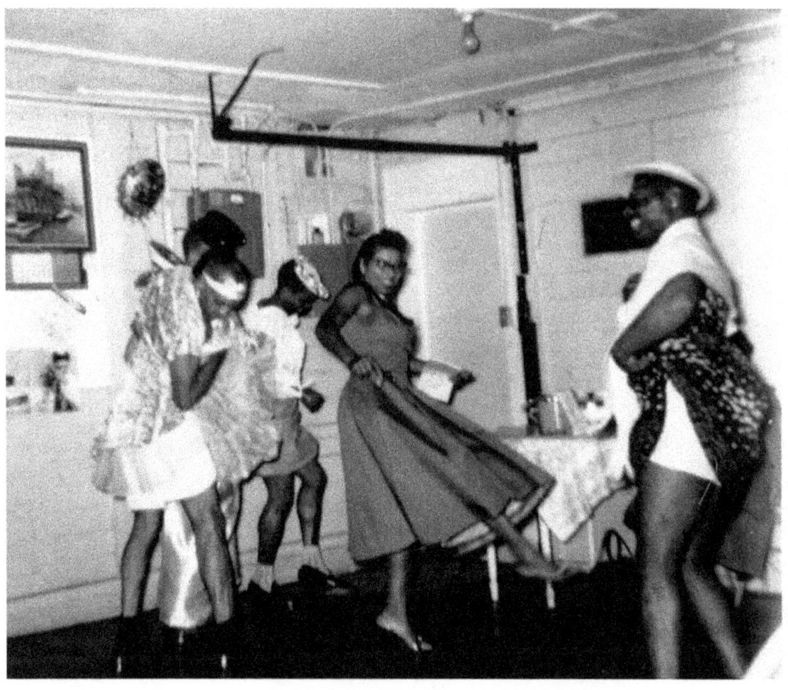

entrapments began. The police, as they did before in the parks, began sending "plain-clothed" officers into queer environments, but with this new law backing them, they began approaching queer people first, because simply being up to meet someone new was now illegal for gay people. The police would purposefully flirt with patrons of the establishments or parks and would even ask the queer individuals if they wanted to go hook up. If the person agreed, they would be arrested; and now there were more charges brought against them and the punishments were more severe. This law effectively made simply existing as a gay individual in the dating scene a criminal offense. Similar anti-LGBTQIA+ laws existed throughout the country, and the ones in NYC stayed on the books until 1967. In that time, more than 50,000 gay men alone were arrested under this 1923 law, and that was only in New York.

❧ ❧ ❧ ❧

The first registered gay, cismale non-profit in the United States was founded in 1924 by a veteran immigrant from Bavaria named Henry Gerber (born Joseph Henry Dittmar, 1892-1972). Gerber emigrated from the German state with his family in 1913, but within four years WWI pulled in the US to the European conflicts his family was trying to avoid. After being sent to an institution when he was twenty-five for being gay, Gerber was given the option of being held as an "enemy alien" or serving in the military: he chose the latter. It was in his three years of active duty in Germany that he was immersed in queer culture and the LGBTQIA+ activism movement that Mangus Hirschfeld and others had started. When he returned to the US after the end of WWI, he was inspired and formed the Society for Human Rights (SHR), even registering it as a non-profit with the state of Illinois. The mission of the group was to create a space for gay people in the world. Membership of SHR was only open to single, gay, cismen, as the group was concerned that their safety would be called into question if other people found out, and this sad statement ended up being true. In the year that SHR was open, Gerber produced the first LGBTQIA+ publication in the US, which was named *Friendship and Freedom*, and devoted much of his time trying to garner support for LGBTQIA+ rights.

Unfortunately, the honesty of Gerber's LGBTQIA+ movement kept people from backing him for fear of being arrested. In July 1925, that fear became a reality for Gerber and his board members, when it was found out that one of their members was a married father, and his wife called social services on the group. Police raided Gerber's home in the middle of the night, and he was arrested. He was tried multiple times, and though all the trials ended in dismissals, the legal cases bankrupted him and cost him his job. He turned to the one job he had before, and re-enlisted in the military, but he never stopped trying to garner equity for LGBTQIA+ people. Gerber would write articles under pseudonyms, and assist up-and-coming queer non-profits with planning and organization, and he did this up until his death in 1972.

The woman nicknamed the "Mother of Blues" and the inspiration for countless creators, from Louis Armstrong to Angela Davis, was bisexual and her name was Gertrude "Ma" Rainey (1886-1939). Rainey was born in Georgia, and from an early age she had a way with music. By the time she was twenty, she was traveling and performing nationally with the Rabbit's Foot Company. After years of performing, she was finally signed to a major label when Paramount contracted her for five years starting in 1923. In her time with the label, she recorded over 100 songs, and some of them openly spoke about her bisexuality, even though queer relationships were illegal at the time. In what is arguably the most overt example, Rainey's "Prove It on Me" is the story of her going out with women and has lines like,

"Went out last night with a crowd of my friends,
They must've been women,
'Cause I don't like no men.
It's true I wear a collar and a tie."

If songs like these aren't lasting proof of Rainey's queer identity, she also ran in the lesbian and bisexual circles of the Harlem Renaissance. In 1925, she was arrested for hosting what was referred to as a "lesbian orgy" at her home in Harlem and had to be bailed out by her musical protégé and presumed lover, Bessie Smith (1894-1937). Those female-loving lyrics even continued with Smith's writings in songs like "The Boy in The Boat" which went,

"When you see two women walking hand in hand,
just look 'em over and try to understand.
They'll go to these parties,
have their lights down low.
Only those parties where women can go."

Eva Kotchever (c.1891-1943) aka Chawa Zloczower aka Eve Adams (Addams) aka Evelyn Adams was a lesbian icon and the United States' modern-day Moll Cutpurse. Kotchever was born in Poland and immigrated to the US in 1912, where she almost immediately found a home with the anarchist movement and its leaders, such as Emma Goldman and Ben Reitman. Her work with the movement put her under the watch of the FBI, and it was only heightened by her running a lesbian tearoom in Chicago, named The Gray Cottage, from 1921-1923. The ending of her Chicago business was not the end of her queer business ventures, and in 1925, after moving to New York City she wrote *Lesbian Love*, which was a culmination of multiple short stories about lesbian relationships, and she opened Eve's Hangout (or Eve Adams Tearoom) which, for the year it was open, was a queer female haven. After complaints to the police, and with the existence of the 1923 anti-LGBTQIA+ law in place, the NYPD sent in a female officer to investigate. According to *Variety Magazine* (again one of the only historical news sources of LGBTQIA+ events), Kotchever's arrest was caused by the following exchange,

> "Evelyn was arrested Thursday night by Policewoman Margaret M. Leonard after the latter claimed she gave her the book at her Washington Square home, entitled 'Lesbian Love.' Miss Adams claims to be the author."

This act of sharing her queer writing was a rebellion, and it was illegal. She was charged with possessing and distributing an indecent book and sentenced to a year in prison. That could have been it for her story, but the authorities could not understand how she was financially able to run her tearoom and publish her book, and began to believe that it was, as written in a July 1926 *Variety* article, run by a "ring of rich cultist" lesbians. In that same article it said that there was a sign outside of the tearoom that read "Men are permitted but not welcome," and when describing the patrons stated,

> "With the opening of Eve's place the big parade of close-cropped women in mannish attire was on again in the Village. In most cases the mannish ladies were accompanied by girls of tender age and some not so tender."

New York's DA tried questioning Kotchever about this supposed wealthy female cult, but she never said a word, or named any other individual who was a part of her circle. This defiance led to her being deported to Europe upon finishing her sentence. After being deported she moved from Poland to France, where she owned a salon named Le Boudoir de l'Amour (the Boudoir of Love). There, queer intellectuals would meet and share ideas and books. She ran the establishment until Nazi forces invaded France, and captured her and her partner, because besides being lesbians they were also Jewish. Kotchever and her partner were sent to Auschwitz, where they became two of the nearly eleven million people the Nazis methodically exterminated over the course of the Holocaust.

❧ ❧ ☙ ☙

In 1926, a song entitled "Masculine Women! Feminine Men!" was released and was meant to be a critique or shaming of sorts, on queer culture, particularly LGBTQIA+ individual's ability to simply not need to fit into the binary. Though this song was meant as a dig, there is such power in reclaiming these hilarious lyrics that attempt to reduce humans to the articles of clothing that they wear. A verse from this gem goes,

> "Now we don't know who is who or even what's what.
> Knickers and trousers, baggy and wide,
> Nobody knows who's walking inside.
> Those Masculine Women, Feminine Men."

It goes on about how women are now smoking, and men are buying cologne, which is yet another example of how even the binary itself has not always existed as it does today. In this truly absurd attempt to bring down queer people, or in any attempt, remember there is freedom and power in understanding that, as RuPaul says, "we're all born naked, and the rest is drag."

Just a "Sewing Circle"

The Queer community and the entertainment world have always been intertwined, from Shakespeare's Sonnet 20 to the word "drag" actually being a stage acronym from the 1870s, meaning "dressed resembling a girl" (which is mistakenly credited to Shakespeare). The reality that the actors are sometimes queer themselves should be no surprise. In fact, when we look at the history of Hollywood, quite a few of the most famous stars were gay, lesbian, bisexual, or even ambisextrous. Queer people, and sexual fluidity in general, were so common between the 1920s and 30s, that they contributed to the Motion Picture Association of America's implementation of the conservative, racist, homophobic Hays Code in 1934 (aka Motion Picture Production Code, 1934-1968, more on this topic later in the book). One of the groups that specifically upset the MPAA, which at the time was effectively just a religious organization, were the queer people who found love without a cisman, or the members of "sewing circles", as they were called. So, to literally draw a picture of some of these relationships, and to honor the groundbreaking hit show *The L Word*, here is a small web of that love, accompanied by a few facts about these queer icons.

**Note: This web could have consisted of hundreds of people from dancers to costume designers to heirs.

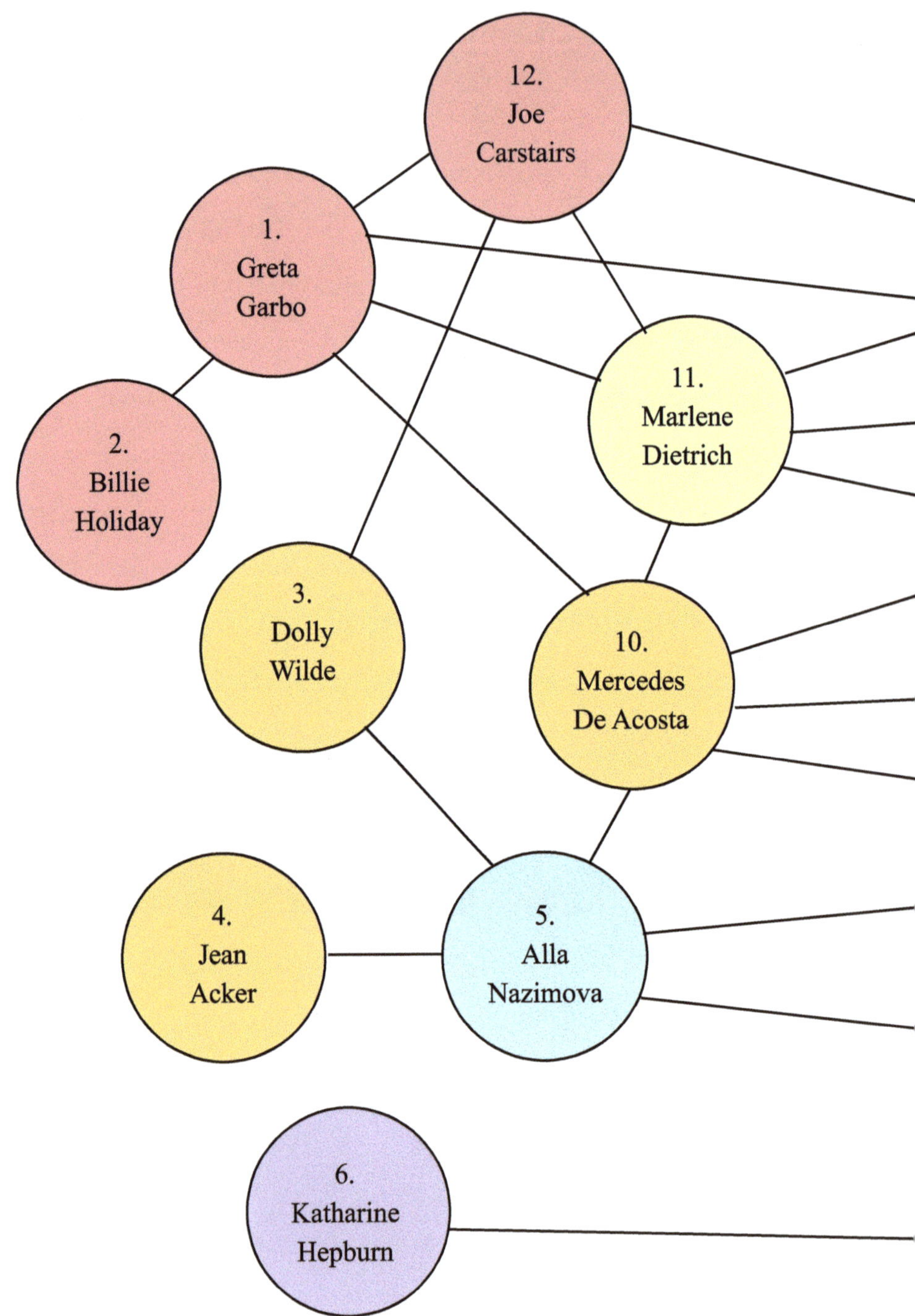
12.
Joe
Carstairs
1.
Greta
Garbo
11.
Marlene
Dietrich
2.
Billie
Holiday
3.
Dolly
Wilde
10.
Mercedes
De Acosta
4.
Jean
Acker
5.
Alla
Nazimova
6.
Katharine
Hepburn

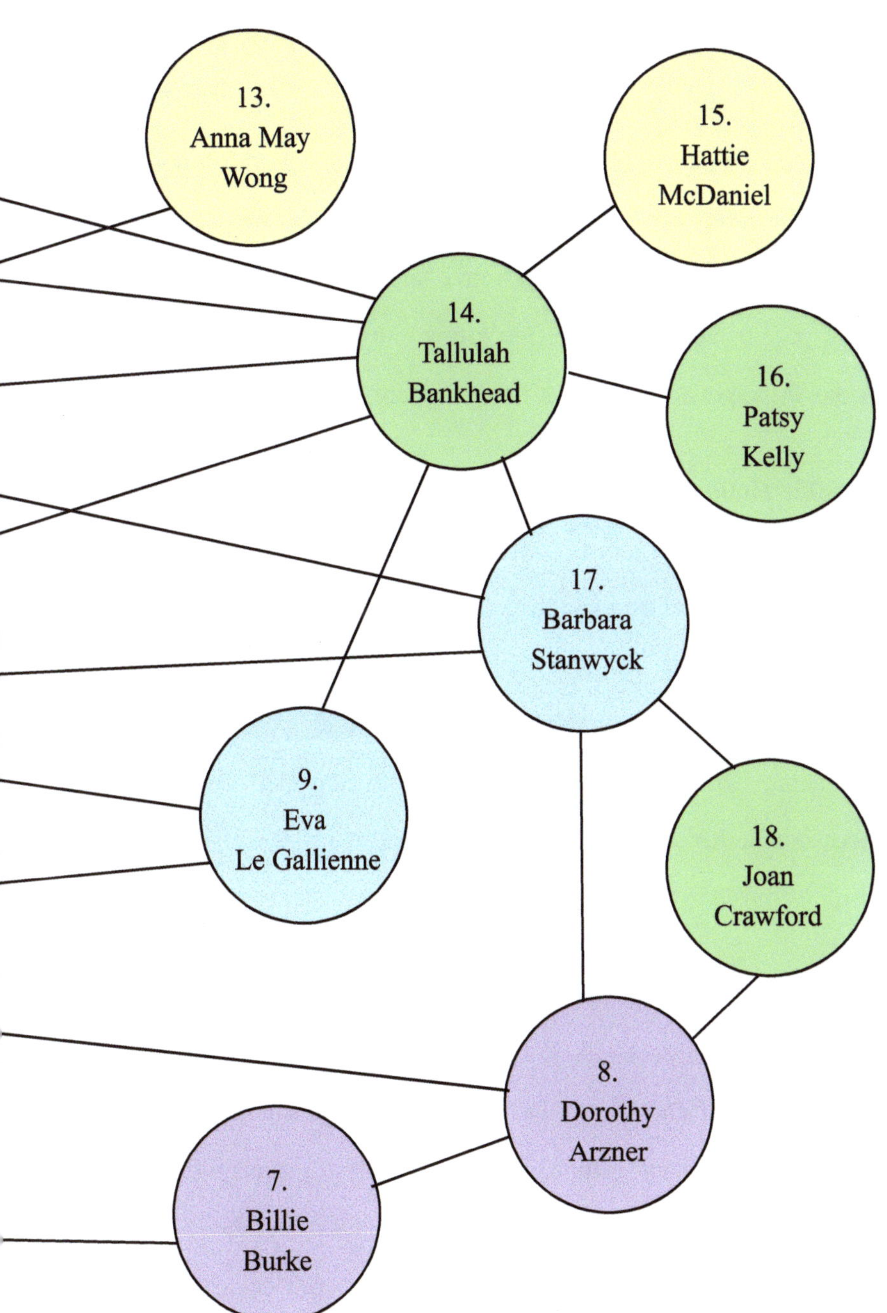
13.
Anna May
Wong
15.
Hattie
McDaniel
14.
Tallulah
Bankhead
16.
Patsy
Kelly
17.
Barbara
Stanwyck
9.
Eva
Le Gallienne
18.
Joan
Crawford
8.
Dorothy
Arzner
7.
Billie
Burke

1. Greta Garbo (1905-1990) - Like several people on this list, Garbo is considered one of the greatest screen actors of all time, though she also has the distinction of being named "The Most Beautiful Woman Who Ever Lived" by Guinness World Records in the 1950s. Her career began in silent film, and she was one of the few who successfully made the move to "talkies." Though she was very private about her life, we know she had relationships with some of the greatest talents of her time, across multiple genders.

2. Billie Holiday (1915-1959) - Holiday began her life as a victim in a cycle of abuse, being trafficked and subsequently arrested for prostitution all before age thirteen, which was due to a still broken and racist system; but she fought to get out of her oppressive situation. She began singing in Harlem nightclubs at fourteen, launching her career, and selling out Carnegie Hall on multiple occasions in her short life. Holiday was and is still a jazz icon, who inspires music to this day.

3. Dolly Wilde (1895-1941) - This last name might seem familiar, and that is because Dolly is the niece of Oscar Wilde, the famed queer author of *The Picture of Dorian Gray*, who was tried in 1895 for "gross indecency" with another man. Dolly is a queer icon in her own right—think of her as the Ellen DeGeneres of her day. She was known for her wit and was a staple in the French salons of time, which was where the "who's who" of the day would mingle.

4. Jean Acker (1893-1978) - An actress whose career began in silent film and lasted decades, Acker is most remembered for her strained marriage to Rudolph Valentino (1895-1926). A marriage that occurred two months after they met, and was rumored to have never been consummated, due to Acker's locking Valentino out of the hotel room on their wedding night. Valentino also had gay love affairs. In his own journal he wrote about a tryst he had with a man he met at the Opera, and said, "we made love like tigers until dawn." In 1923, when their divorce was finalized, Acker met Chloe Carter, whom she remained with for over fifty years until her death in 1978.

5. Alla Nazimova (1879-1945) - Credited with originating the term "sewing circle," which referred to the "underground" network of

Alla Nazimova, 1927

queer hook-ups and relationships that occurred among the women in Hollywood, Nazimova is considered one of the most influential people of it all. She was never one to shy away from being herself, and so as a bisexual woman, she openly dated women while being married to men. If breaking sexuality boundaries was not enough, she was also one of the first women to own and run a production company in Hollywood.

6. Katharine Hepburn (1907-2003) - An icon transcending queerness, holding the record for most wins for Best Actress at the Academy Awards to this day, Hepburn was known for her independence in an age when women were assumed to be obedient. When she was a child, she shaved her head and wanted to be called Jimmy, and that tomboy attitude never left her. She dated men and women throughout her life, her first, most notable relationship with a woman, being Laura Harding, who was the heir to the American Express fortune.

7. Billie Burke (1884-1970) - Burke, who had a career from radio to talking-pictures, is best known as Glinda the Good Witch in the 1939 movie, *The Wizard of Oz*, which quite literally makes her a "friend of Dorothy."

8. Dorothy Arzner (1897-1979) - The definition of a barrier breaker, Arzner went through life openly, publicly living with her partner Marion Morgan for over forty years. She was one of the only female directors at the time, directing twenty films, her first in 1922 (*Blood and Sand*, though it was uncredited), and became the first female member of the Director's Guild Association, not to mention being credited with inventing the boom microphone: she had attached a mic to a fishing pole. To further add to her legacy, she was also a mentor to Francis Ford Coppola.

9. Eva Le Gallienne (1899-1991) - Le Gallienne wore many hats in her life: actor, author, director, manager; and she wore them all well. She is remembered as one of the best to play Peter Pan on Broadway, as well as founding the Civic Repertory Theatre, which led to the creation of Off-Broadway shows. In queer history, she is known for being involved in a high-profile affair with another actor, Josephine Hutchinson, whose husband then preceded to divorce her, and essentially name Le Gallienne in the paperwork as the cause of the divorce. Though this led to a brief dark period of her life, she was always quite proud of her love for women, saying, "People hate what they don't understand and try to destroy it. Only try to keep yourself clear and do not allow that destructive force to spoil something that to you is simple, natural, and beautiful."

10. Mercedes De Acosta (1892-1968) - A poet, screenwriter and prolific lover in the queer community, De Acosta was to Hollywood and Broadway what Papi was to *The L Word*. Her home in

Brentwood was the party house among the gay Hollywood elite in the 1930s-40s, and her list of partners seems almost endless. She was writing a memoir called *Here Lies the Heart* before she died, which outlined her life and all her most tantalizing encounters. Though the work will forever remain unfinished, and some details have been debated, it is still a standout in first-hand queer stories for the time.

Marlene Dietrich, c. 1930s

11. Marlene Dietrich (1901-1992) - German-born Dietrich was said to have energy that had masculinity to attract women, and sexuality to attract men, and that all can be seen in her deep gaze, coupled with her signature tux, top hat, and long cigarette holder. Besides being a queer legend, who took part in the heyday of 1920s gay Berlin, and had affairs with anyone and everyone she felt like, she also was a vocal anti-Nazi who turned down Hitler's request to star in a propaganda film. She also donated her money and time to support US soldiers through the USO, as well as refugees escaping from war torn Europe. She publicly renounced her German citizenship during WWII, in part because she was a woman with a platform, who was ready to take on the world, and did.

12. Joe Carstairs (1900-1993) - Carstairs went by Joe for most of his life, "despising" the use of his birth name, presented in male associated clothing, and wore a fake mustache while in his home; so he/him pronouns will be used here, in place of she/her which is typically used in reference to him. Carstairs was the cigar-smoking, tattooed heir to the Standard Oil fortune, and in true heir fashion, he was a Casanova, owned private islands, and was a world-renowned speed boat racer. Though Carstairs was a known romancer, he lost his true love, Ruth Baldwin, in 1937; and for the rest of his life, he carried around a doll that Baldwin gave him, named Lord Tod Wadley, even being cremated with it. Something else that he did in his life was write poetry under the pseudonym Hans Bernstein. One poem that truly shows the internal thoughts of Carstairs, is *Perversities of Mankind*, which goes: “There's / The / man / Who / Wants / A Skirt / And / The girl / Who / Wears / A shirt / Even / Fish / That / Want / To fly -- / I / Wonder why?"

13. Anna May Wong (1905-1961) - Wong is considered the first female Chinese American actor to gain international success but being the first never mattered more than her integrity. She was once passed over for the lead role, which was supposed to be a Chinese character, for a white actor (besides overt racism, this was also due to the racist Hays Code, which did not allow for interracial couples to be shown on screen, and the lead opposite was already cast as a white man). When MGM tried offering her a secondary character in the film, she turned it down flat out based on principle.

14. Tallulah Bankhead (1902-1968) - A woman ahead of her time, there is no better quote from Bankhead than, “My father warned me about men and booze, but never said anything about women and cocaine.” She was outspoken and open about her sexuality and sexual experiences, something that was considered a no-no at the time and had her marked by the Hays Code as “unsuitable for the public,” but it makes Bankhead one badass legend now. She was self-described as ambisextrous, which can be used interchangeably with bisexual, for her purposes, and she rivals De Acosta for the pinnacle of the female queer world of Old Hollywood.

15. Hattie McDaniel (1895-1952) - Icon is an understatement for McDaniel, who is not only the first Black woman to sing on the radio, but also the first Black *person* to win an Academy Award. When she attended the 1939 award ceremony, McDaniel was only allowed in as a favor, had to sit at the back of the room, and was not allowed to attend the after party. This was all after she was not allowed to go to the premiere of the film, *Gone with the Wind*, in Atlanta. To put into perspective just how incredible McDaniel's win was, it took over fifty years for another Black woman to win an Oscar, of any kind (Whoopi Goldberg for *Ghost* in 1991).

16. Patsy Kelly (1910-1981) - The personal assistant, friend, and sometimes lover of Tallulah Bankhead, Kelly was an out lesbian actor, who openly talked about her relationships with women, and her desire to never get married. She was close friends with Gene Malin, a gay drag performer who made it big during the pansy craze (more on that soon) and was in the car with him when he had his fatal accident.

17. Barbara Stanwyck (1907-1990) - One of the favorites of director Cecil B. DeMille (you know, "Mr. DeMille, I'm ready for my close-up", that guy), and the highest-paid woman in Hollywood in 1944, Stanwyck was a staple of radio, TV, and movies for over sixty years. Besides being part of movies by acting in them, her life also inspired film; it is believed that her marriage to Frank Fay was the muse for *A Star is Born* (that same one written by Dorothy Parker and remade with Gaga). Though she was married twice to men, both are believed to be lavender marriages (more on this in a bit), and her partner for over thirty years, until her death, was her publicist, Helen Ferguson.

18. Joan Crawford (c.1908-1977) - Crawford began her career using her birth name, Lucille LeSueur, but was told it sounded "fake", so in an ironic twist, in 1925 a contest was held to "Name the Star" and give her a fake name that sounded real. After a few hiccups, Joan Crawford was born (this "birth year" we know, unlike her actual birth year which could be from 1904-1908). Always a woman to make her own path, and care very little about the implications of that, she said that no one made her a star: "Joan Crawford became a star because Joan Crawford decided to become a star." She never admitted to her numerous lesbian-leaning affairs, but there is an abundance of personal accounts to support the truth, most notably her daughter's memoir, *Mommie Dearest.*

❧ ❧ ❧ ❧

Beginning in the late 1920s a period in history called the "pansy craze" began and lasted until the end of prohibition and the implementation of the Hays Code in the film industry. Drag balls and shows were a staple of the LGBTQIA+ community and had been for decades, and they were mostly hosted in underground speakeasies, which meant that when the US government banned alcohol, the queer establishments were already ahead of the game. The gays had alcohol, and so when the cis/het world realized, they found a new level of "tolerance" for us. Drag performers became the new trend and cis/het society deemed drag appropriate within the context of parties and entertainment. This is stated specifically because the laws surrounding LGBTQIA+ people and their appearance were not amended, and many drag performers and trans individuals were arrested during this time. One such arrest is noted in a 1929 *Variety* article titled "'Boys' Powder Puff Missing-Dismissed." The article tells of the arrest of two drag queens who were performers at the Everglades Club, a well-known queer bar. It tells of the "upset" they caused in court in their dresses,

> "Both were attired in women's clothes. George wore a Spanish shawl and beautiful flaming red dress, while Louis was similarly attired."

It truly seems as though the writer was quite taken with George. Unlike George and Louis, a few queer performers became household names, like Gene Malin (1908-1933) and Karyl Norman (1897-1947), but the fame was short-lived. When prohibition ended in 1933, part of the law concerning alcohol stated that it could only be served in "orderly" establishments, and guess what the cis/het world deemed disorderly? Queer establishments. As well, in almost direct reaction to the pansy craze, the Hays Code was enacted. The Hays Code was semi-based around New York's Wales Padlock Law,

which made it illegal for any play or performance to "depict or deal with the subject of sex degeneracy, or sex perversion." What was considered a perversion? Queerness. The Hays Code went a step further, applying to all films and television produced in the US and effectively turning the film industry into a conservative, religious machine. The code was in affect for more than thirty years and besides banning any "sexual perversion," the code also banned interracial couples from appearing on screen, "lustful" kissing, sympathy for criminals, and people lying in the same bed. That last one can be seen in classics like *I Love Lucy*, where married couple

Ricky and Lucy do not share a bed, despite the actors also being married off screen. In fact, when Lucy got pregnant in real life the network almost cancelled the show. When they did not, Lucille Ball became the first person to be shown pregnant on television in a scripted show.

As the Motion Picture Association of America started enforcing the Hays Code more and more in the mid-1930s, the production companies of Hollywood began enforcing their morality clauses with their actors. In old Hollywood, actors would be signed to a specific production company, whether it was MGM, Universal, or Warner Brothers, and they would work exclusively for that company. These contracts meant that the actors couldn't leave and film somewhere else, and it also meant that the companies could fully control the actor's image. When it came to morality clauses, the studios would use these to keep actors from things like doing drugs, gambling, or being queer. Many queer entertainers were forced into what were known as lavender marriages, which were straight-appearing relationships for the public eye, something of the modern-day beard (today's coded phrase for the same situation). Some of these lavender marriages were made up of a gay man and a lesbian woman, others of one queer individual and a seemingly in-the-dark partner, but all of them were publicity stunts to pander to homophobic public opinion. Rock Hudson (1925-1985), the handsome leading man who starred opposite James Dean and Elizabeth Taylor in *Giant* (1956), entered into a lavender marriage in 1955 to stop a story about his gay identity from being published. On the opposite side of the spectrum, actor William Haines (1900-1973) gave up his entire acting career when MGM tried to force him into a lavender marriage. Not willing to give up his partner, Jimmie Shields, Haines gave up Hollywood and the two of them opened an interior design business together and spent almost fifty years as loving spouses.

❧ ❧ ❧ ❧

In the 1930s, lesbians in Paris developed a covert way to signal their queerness to each other by wearing a monocle, and so one of the most famous lesbian bars of the time was called Le Monocle. The club opened sometime in the late 1920s and was run by a tuxedo-wearing lesbian who went by the name Lulu de Montparnasse. The club was known for its suit-wearing lesbian staff and being the go-to location for the who's who of the non-cismale queer world. Marlene Dietrich frequented Le Monocle and even began an on-again-off-again love affair that lasted decades with Frede (1914-1976), one of the entertainers at the club. French author, and open bisexual, Colette (1873-1954) confirmed this lesbian style in her famed *Le Pur et l'Impur (The Pure and the Impure,* 1932*)* describing how lesbians "often affecting a monocle and a white carnation in the buttonhole," and in almost all Brassaï's photographs of Le Monocle there is just that. Just as with the drag balls of Paris, Brassaï photographed the private lives of the patrons inside Le Monocle, from group photos to intimate couples around a table, and they exist as proof of the club that the Nazis destroyed when they invaded France (common theme in this book).

**As an extra note, Colette and one of her partners, Max de Morny (born Mathilde de Morny, 1863-1944) once put on a show at the Moulin Rouge where they kissed on stage, and it caused such an uproar and scandal that they had to hide their relationship from the public for the next five years. Her life was turned into a movie entitled *Colette* (2018) starring Kiera Knightley. Though some liberties were taken, and they cast a ciswoman as a transman, it truly is a great story that shows representation of a bisexual star.

Note the monocle, c. 1920

There is a chance that the first time "Live, Laugh, Love" was printed was not on the wall of a white lady's beach house, but actually on a flyer for a queer event that was known as "Lady Austin's Camp Boys." In December 1932, after police were tipped off about one of the parties (no thanks to the flyers, which are still held in the UK's National Archives, as they were formerly evidence), two officers, one wearing a suit, the other in a dress, were able to gain entry Lady Austin's drag event in Holland Park, London. The officers stayed all night and took part in the dances of the "queenies" and "kings," as the patrons were called based upon their choice of attire. As the morning hours rolled in, the party was raided and the head queen herself, Lady Austin, came to the defense of her guests. When the police accused her of running a brothel, she defiantly stated that none of the events were for profit and asked the police, "What harm are we doing? You don't understand our love." The courts convicted twenty of the sixty guests of crimes involving "diverse lewd, scandalous, bawdy and obscene performances and practices," and through it all Lady Austin handled it in true drag queen fashion, with her sassy quip stated in the police report, "Oh, dear, this trouble would be obviated if they made our love legal."

Queer people have always been willing to fight for our liberation, as well as that of those around us, and during the Holocaust and the Nazi's invasion of Europe, it was no different. Claude Cahun

(1894-1954) and their partner Marcel Moore (1892-1972), both non-binary artists who left a legacy of self-portraits of gender expression, happened to also be passionate anti-Nazis. When German troops invaded their home of Jersey (an island off the coast of France) in 1937, they began to use their art to sabotage. They would translate BBC reports of Nazi crimes into German and write the reports in poems and rhymes, signed "the soldier with no name," to create conspiracy in the troops. The pair would then infiltrate the Nazi meetings, dressed as soldiers and plant their writings. They did this until 1944 when they were arrested and sentenced to death, but they were lucky and the island was liberated, and their sentences were never carried out. Willem Ardoneus (1894-1943) was another hero of the war in his home of the Netherlands, when he gave his life to protect thousands of lives of his neighbors. Ardoneus worked with an underground network to create forged identification cards for Jewish people and other targets of the Nazi's attacks. One obstacle the group faced were the records held at the Municipal Office for Population Registration, which was a building containing copies of everyone's ID. These original copies could be compared to the fakes and clearly discredit them. Ardoneus and his cronies made the decision to bomb the building while it was closed, to avoid loss of life. So, on March 27, 1943, they carried out their plan and were able to destroy 800,000 ID cards, but within weeks Ardoneus was arrested. He refused to give up his partners and was sentenced to death. His last wish was for a pink shirt to wear, and his final words were, “let it be known homosexuals by definition are not cowards.”

In 1939, a Cantonese-language film was released entitled *Nu ren shi jie* (English title: *It's a Women's World*), which followed thirty-six different women and their personal, yet relatable, harsh realities of being a woman in society. The film was co-written/directed by a legend in her own right, Esther Eng (born Ng Kam-ha, 1914-1970). Besides being considered the first female director of Chinese descent in Hollywood, she also lived her life openly as a lesbian. Eng began her career in film at just nineteen years old when she co-produced *Heartaches* (1935), which is considered one of the premiere Chinese American films to be made, and from there she propelled to fame. She traveled from San Francisco to Hong Kong in 1936 to expand her family's production company, Kwong Ngai Talking Pictures Company (Cathay Pictures Ltd.), internationally. While in China, the media fawned over her, idolizing her clean-cut suits, her way with film, and her number of affairs with her "bosom friends" and "good sisters," as the papers would call them. She stayed in China producing, writing, directing, and distributing films until 1939 when the outbreak of WWII spurred her to return to the US, but it did not stop her from creating. Eng would create what are thought to be some of the most iconic Cantonese language films to come out of Hollywood, including *Golden Gate Girl* (1941), which is actually Bruce Lee's debut film, where he played an infant assigned female at birth. After she left the creation side of film in 1949, she ran a movie distribution company and opened the Bo Bo

Restaurant in NYC, where she quietly lived the remainder of her legendary life.

❧ ❧ ☙ ☙

To say Josephine Baker (1906-1975, and pictured above c.1924) was accomplished would be an understatement; she was the first Black woman to star in a major motion picture, received the Croix de guerre, the Rosette de la Résistance, and was made a Chevalier of the Légion d'honneur by General Charles de Gaulle (which are some of the highest honors a French civilian can receive), and though she lived with her sexuality hidden and was sometimes vocally anti-queer (homophobia is a common armor for those who are deeply repressed), she was very much a bisexual woman. Her life began in turmoil, a survivor of abuse and sexual assault all before the age of thirteen, but Baker was not going to let the world define her by the abuse she faced, so she used her talents in dance and entertainment to find a way out. By fifteen, Baker had lived more of a life than most do in their entirety; she had been married twice, had several affairs with women, and began traveling with a theater company, which was a job she got thanks to one of her "lady lovers," Blues singer Clara Smith (1894-1935). Though Baker saw mild success in America's vaudeville scene, racism and segregation were holding her back, so at nineteen she moved to Paris and experienced what she called in her own words her "first big break." She became an instant sensation, a star among the stars really, drawing admiration from names like Ernest Hemingway and Pablo Picasso, and having romantic trysts with Colette (French novelist mentioned prior), Frida Kahlo (1907-1954), Bessie Allison Buchanan (1902-1980, the first Black woman elected to the NY State Assembly), and Ada "Bricktop" Smith (1894-1984), who was an American Jazz legend, cafe/club culture godmother, and Baker's mentor. Baker was successful for years: she starred in her first major film, the silent hit *Siren of Tropics* in 1927, and began touring all over Europe, though she always considered Paris her home. When

France declared war on Germany in 1937, the Deuxième Bureau (French military intelligence) approached Baker with the chance to be a spy, and so she became part of the network of entertainers who were WWII spies (which was a tactic used by the Allies and Axis' alike). She would gather intel at the events where she hosted or performed, charming foreign Axis officials and finding out those key confidential details to help the French Resistance during WWII (this use of women as spies during the war was a huge information gathering effort, particularly with sex workers). With her fame supporting her, she was able to freely travel around Europe during wartime travel lockdowns, which allowed her to pass messages between Allied powers, and led to her winning numerous awards for her service to France. After the war, in her personal life she adopted twelve children from all over the world, which she called the Rainbow Tribe, with her fourth husband, Jo Bouillon (1908-1984), who was also bisexual. Her passion for action did not fade however, and she continued fighting in the cause for civil rights, becoming one of the faces of the movement. Baker refused to perform at segregated venues, had an honorary lifetime membership to the NAACP, and was the only official woman speaker at Martin Luther King Jr.'s March on Washington (yes, the "I Have a Dream" March on Washington). Baker had to get special permission from the sitting Attorney General, Robert F. Kennedy, to even enter the US and give her speech, since she had her visa revoked during McCarthy's absurd red scare. Her speech discusses the racism she faces, even with her fame, and she ends it mentioning her meeting set with the President and this quote,

> "You know I have always taken the rocky path. I never took the easy one, but as I get older, and as I knew I had the power and the strength, I took that rocky path, and I tried to smooth it out a little. I wanted to make it easier for you. I want you to have a chance at what I had. But I do not want you to have to run away to get it."

With the end of Prohibition, queer establishments saw an onslaught of harassment from the newly formed state/local "liquor authorities," whose mission it was to avoid the "saloon" atmosphere that had led to the 18th amendment. As mentioned previously, these "liquor authorities" regulated the selling of alcohol (still seen today in Alcohol Beverage Control or ABC stores), issuing liquor licenses for bars and restaurants, and monitoring the businesses after the fact. In New York the agency is called the State Liquor Authority (SLA), and they believed that establishments that served alcohol could not be "disorderly," and by that they meant the patrons could not be users of drugs, homeless, gamblers, sex workers, or queer (this was a similar theme amongst most of the "liquor authorities"). In 1939, after years of raids, arrests, attacks, and closures, one of the bars that had their license revoked decided to take a stand and sued the SLA. Gloria's was a bar in Murray Hill known for being an LGBTQIA+ hangout, and after undercover SLA officers revoked their liquor license for multiple queer incidents (the report is riddled with queer slurs), Gloria's sued, becoming one of the first cases in a US court to fight for queer peoples' right to simply exist in a space together. Gloria's argued that not only was the SLA not educated enough to identify LGBTQIA+ people (they brought scientific medical backing from the Committee for the Study of Sex Variants, which was a psychiatrist-led LGBTQIA+ group in NY), but that there was no rule specifically stating serving queer people was illegal, and that if the patrons were not acting "disorderly" there was nothing wrong with queer spaces. As this was an arm of the government itself, the decision did not go in the bar's favor, and it further cemented the SLA's overreaching attacks on queer establishments over the next three decades. Those same attacks would create a powder keg and lead to the Stonewall Riots.

❧ ❧ ☙ ☙

World War II might have been at least two years longer and seen 14 million more lives lost, had it not been for Alan Turing (1912-1954) and the work of his fellow codebreakers at Hut 8, a part of the UK government's code and cypher school. Turing had degrees from Oxford and Princeton (one being a PhD), helped develop improvements to the bombe method used to crack the Nazi's enigma machine, created Banburismus to decrypt U-boat messages, and led in the creation and gave his name to Turingery, which helped the Allies crack some of the most sensitive enemy correspondences, all by the time he was thirty. Besides helping shorten the war and saving millions of lives, Turing is also considered one of the founding humans of computer science. Prior to the war he had worked on the universal Turing machine and the Church-Turing theory, which are considered to be the core of the theory of computation and development of algorithms (the basis for all computer algorithms). After the war, he continued his research and during 1945-1947 designed ACE (Automatic Computing Engine), which is effectively the OG computer. With all these contributions to society (not that it is needed), in 1952, after Turing had contacted police because he was robbed, the police ignored the robbery and promptly arrested him because his boyfriend was in the house with him. Turing was given the option of jail or a year of hormone therapy to "reduce his libido" (injections of diethylstilbestrol, an estrogen shot), and he picked the latter. Due to his criminal convictions, he lost his government job and could no longer work in the US (more on that in a few), but he was able to keep his teaching career at Manchester for the remaining two years of his life. Turing died from cyanide poisoning in 1954, and though it was ruled as a suicide, there is much speculation about this, from the conspiracies about government assassination due to the lack of a note to an alternate, accidental method of ingestion being present in his lab. Accidental or not, the world lost a genius whose work is still highly regarded and studied to this day, and in 2013 he was officially pardoned by Queen Elizabeth II (after years of petitioning and activists' fighting). A final addition to Turing's legacy is that his pardon sparked the 2017 law offering retroactive pardons for queer men convicted under the same anti-gay law as he was.

❧ ❧ ❧ ❧

A League of Their Own (1992) got a lot of things right about the All-American Girls Professional Baseball League (AAGPBL): the Rockford Peaches did win the most titles, the "uniforms" were short, one piece skirt-tunics that made no sense for the sport, and that theme song they sang was actually the song of the league, but something the film really missed the mark on was the large concentration of lesbian and bisexual women in the league. In fact, the reason that the uniforms look like a straight cismales idea of women playing baseball (besides the fact that a straight cismale designed them) is because they were intentionally meant to "feminize" the players. AAGPBL founder, Philip K. Wrigley (gum/ candy and Cubs owner) believed women playing sports were too "masculine" and the athletes needed to "play like a man, look like a lady." The rules for the players' appearance went further, outlawing anything that could be perceived as masculine or queer, including banning short haircuts all together, a rule that saw many players lose their spot in the league. Josephine "JoJo" D'Angelo was cut just a year into her contract for a haircut deemed "butchy." The players were made to go to charm school and hide any aspect of their queer identities, but that did not stop them from finding love and relationships with each other and other women, as discussed in Netflix's 2020 documentary, *A Secret Love*, which is about the beautiful, life-long love story of player, Terry Donahue and her partner Pat Henschel and how they dealt with consistent homophobia from the start, but fought through it to live their lives together for more than seventy years.

19 A F 14

19 A F 14

Lucy Hicks Anderson (1886-1954) knew who she was from a young age, and she was not going to allow anyone to try and tell her differently, whether it was her parents or the US government. Anderson was assigned male at birth, but by the time she could communicate with words, she told her parents she was a girl, and her name was Lucy. Her parents brought her to their local doctor in Kentucky, who instructed them to allow her to just live as herself, so Anderson's life of authenticity began. She went to school presenting as herself, and by twenty she was a talented chef and able to leave her hometown for her next chapter. Anderson married her first husband in 1920 and they moved to Oxnard, CA, where she would blossom as an event planning, socialite, madam. She divorced her first husband after nine years and was able to buy her own space to open her bordello, which she successfully ran for years. In 1945, after only a year of being married to her second husband, a retired soldier, there was an STD outbreak among the sailors on the local base that was "traced" back to her establishment. The investigation led to doctors examining all the women that worked there including Anderson, upon which she and her husband were arrested and charged with perjury for "lying" on their marriage certificate. Anderson argued that she did not lie about anything because she was a woman, and boldly stated in court, "I have lived, dressed, acted just what I am, a woman." Though both she and her husband were found guilty and banned from the city of Oxnard for ten years, this makes her the first LGBTQIA+ person to go on record in court defending queer people's right to marriage. She was a Black, transfeminine sex worker (which is a theme seen throughout this book). After the trial and jail sentences, the couple moved to LA, where they lived quietly together until Anderson passed away in 1954.

yours sincerely

Chapter Four: End of a War, Beginning of a Revolution (1946-1969)

Vada that bona vardering omee holding the gamp; she's on the team and was the trade of the week for the cruising seafood. No that sentence was not a typo, it is Polari, the secret language of the queer subculture that began to form in the UK around the 1800s and saw its heyday in the 1950s. Certain aspects of Polari derived from a few other slang languages, in particular, Parlyaree, a language spoken by typically lower-income people who worked in traveling jobs, Lingua Franca, specifically the "common language" used by sailors and merchants, and Thieves Cant, which dates back to at least the 1600s. Other parts of Polari come from standard slang methods such as, back-slang (words spelled backwards), repetition, alliteration, blends (combining words), rhymes, and pararhymes. The language was used to build community and allow LGBTQIA+ people to identify each other, as well as creating safety in public spaces, where being or speaking about queerness could mean arrest or worse. In the language cismales were referred to using female pronouns, so in that way if someone were to overhear a gay man speaking about his love interest, the prying ears would assume they were hearing a cis/het conversation. By the 1950s, due to World War II and soldiers (mainly young cismales) traveling through Europe, the use of Polari had expanded beyond the UK and began being used in the US, Australia, and throughout Europe. As with most marginalized groups and their traditions, parts of this language were absorbed into mainstream culture, even being used in the UK's popular 1960s radio show *Round the Horne*. Some of these words that found their origins in Polari are still used today, like "butch," "trade," and "camp" (as in the 2019 Met Gala theme), and it is in those modern uses that Polari and queer culture is yet again embedded and intertwined with mainstream society. Oh, and that first sentence says: "Look at that good looking man holding the umbrella; he's gay and was the hook-up of the week for the cruising sailors" (queer use of "cruising").

Self: A Study in Ethics and Endocrinology by Michael Dillon (1915-1962) was published in 1946, and it is one of the first works to analyze the transgender experience using a multi-layered approach, from the perspective of an actual transgender individual. Dillon was born into an affluent family that held a baronetcy in Ireland, something that would end up catapulting his quiet, reserved life into the limelight. From childhood, Dillon always knew who he was and never attempted to hide his authentic self, and with the advent of gender-confirming medical treatments, the new Oxford alumnus began hormone therapy in 1939. As with queer people even now, there was a severe lack of available education around his identity, so Dillon sought to create an education for himself and in 1945 enrolled back in school to become a doctor, which was right around the time that he also met Sir Harold Gillies (1882-1960). Gillies was a surgeon who helped develop new skin and tissue grafting techniques to help badly injured soldiers during both world wars and is considered one of the founders of the field of plastic surgery. Over the course of the next nine years, Dillion underwent seventeen surgeries at Rooksdown House, and was able to receive the gender-affirming care that he needed in his journey to be his authentic self, and he happens to be the first known transman to do so. While Dillon was going through this nine-year process, he met Roberta Cowell (1918-2011), a transwoman who was inspired by his work, *Self,* and with whom he fell madly in love. Cowell was also seeking assistance in her medical transition, but was blocked by UK's transphobic rules surrounding orchiectomy, and so as is common among people who do not have access to appropriate medical care, the pair decided to do it themselves. Dillon, who was a year away from officially being a doctor, performed the operation for Cowell, and this opened the door to allow her to receive the remaining operations that she needed for herself. Where Dillon was private about his identity, Cowell shared her story with the media and became a minor celebrity, which created a rift between the pair. Dillon became a Navy surgeon and lived quietly until May 1958 when a discrepancy between two peerage books (highly detailed accounts of all the titles and who the heirs to the titles are in the United Kingdom/Ireland) caused a media frenzy. Burke's 1956 book listed Dillion's deadname, while Debrett's 1954 edition had recognized Dillon's real name. It is more than likely that someone outed Dillon (among their friends it is thought to have been Cowell, herself), as the likelihood of someone finding this inconsistency on their own is like finding one specific needle in a needle stack. The attention was more than Dillon could handle, so he left for India and joined a Buddhist community, where he worked on becoming a monk until he passed away. Cowell, who was a spitfire pilot in WWII and a champion race car driver, led a life of sensation and readily shared her story with the world. Both of these transgender ancestors left autobiographies, Cowell's entitled *An Autobiography: Roberta Cowell's Story* (1954) and Dillon's, published fifty-five years after his death, called *Out of the Ordinary* (2017).

Many people know about the "red scare" and Senator Joseph McCarthy's (1908-1957) witch hunt for communists who had "infiltrated" the government, but another group of people that McCarthy and the government deemed a "security risk" were LGBTQIA+ people, and this operation was known as the "lavender scare." In 1947, around the height of the Cold War and backed by President Truman, McCarthy and his counterparts in the State Department began codifying rules about who could work for them, and the banned characteristics list included that age-old favorite, "sexual perversion." In the first three years of this process, nearly 2,000 applicants were denied federal jobs due to accusations of being queer. To further draw *The Crucible* (1953) reference (Arthur Miller's Salem witch trial play that was an allegory for McCarthyism), co-worker accusations of queer "behavior" among active staff increased by 1,100%. In case there is any doubt that this was a government-fueled attack on LGBTQIA+ individuals and our ability to have secure and stable work, in 1950 Republican Nebraska State Representative Arthur L. Miller (not to be confused with *The Crucible* author) took to the House floor to address "Homosexuals in the Government." In this slur-riddled, homophobic tirade, Miller talks about how queer people have "odd words in their vocabulary." Unknowingly referring to Polari, he ranted, "You will find those people using the words as, 'He is a fish.'" (Please note that "fish" is no longer an appropriate term to use). Miller continued about his guess at the number of queer people in DC, and more specifically working in government positions,

> "We learned two years ago that there were around four thousand homosexuals in the District. The Police Department the other day said there were between five and six thousand in

> Washington who are active and that seventy-five percent were in Government employment."

It is in this type of fear-mongering environment that, of course, there is an increase in accusations. If it is not the "you or me" mentality, it becomes a means to tear down an opponent (a version of queerbaiting). The people who were accused of being queer were interrogated, their personal lives were invaded, and in most cases, their reputations were ruined, and their jobs were lost (whether they were actually queer or not). This set the stage for President Eisenhower's 1953 Executive Order 10450 which basically said if the government thinks you could be blackmailed, then you can be fired. The number of people who were terminated for being LGBTQIA+ far eclipses the number who were fired for being a member of the Communist party, and it is not hard to see why.

The gay and community was still searching for a word that they could collectively agree upon as their umbrella term, and after the end of WWII there was a shift to use "homophile" in place of "homosexual." Unsurprisingly, homophile, like most Western LGBTQIA+ terms, was originally coined in 1924 by a German physician (he was a problematic gay man who was a Nazi, and he was killed on the Night of the Long Knives). The reason that the word began gaining popularity almost twenty-five years after its original entrance into the world, was due in large part to queer activism. The need to organize and collectively fight for the rights of the community meant the community needed a "label" to stand behind, and they wanted the focus to pull away from physical sex (homosexual was the most common) and focus on the emotional love and relationship aspect, which was meant to show cis/het society that queer people were "just like them." With the word homophile the goal was achieved: both parts are from Greek, *homo* meaning "same," and *phile* meaning "love." One of the first groups involved in the homophile movement was Danish activist Axel Axgil's Kredsen af 1948 (Circle of 1948), a gay lobby group working towards equity on all levels through policy and law change (now a national organization under the name LGBT Denmark). From there, the movement spread through Europe and by 1951 the International Committee for Sexual Equality (ICSE) was formed and consisted of activist groups from Italy, the Netherlands, Denmark, the UK, Germany, Switzerland, and later the US. The group began to coordinate their fight, even sending a letter to the United Nations demanding equality for all gay people. The ICSE operated until 1963, when there was again a shift in how queer people needed to fight for liberation, and the homophile term and movement (which focused on assimilation of queer people into straight society) faded and was absorbed into what would become the queer revolution.

That one random bit of trivia that everyone knows that says, "10% of the population is gay," actually comes from famed biologist, psychologist, and zoologist turned sexologist, the Western bisexual, polyamorous revolutionary, Alfred Kinsey (1894-1956). His 1948 book, *Sexual Behavior in the Human Male*, was compiled from over 5,300 in-person interviews with white people assigned male at birth and it pulled the curtain from the mainstream world's (specifically the US) rigid view on sexual experience and showed the very queer wizard behind it all (Dorothy reference, get it?). Kinsey was a man of many passions: he was a talented pianist, avid botanist, one of the first Eagle Scouts ever, and intrigued by all things nature and science. He received his doctorate from Harvard, where he taught briefly before being hired to teach at Indiana University (IU) in 1920. It was here that Kinsey's focus shifted from the study of sex and sexual identity in animals, to humans, and it all started when he began teaching "Marriage and Family," in 1938. The class, which was offered to married IU seniors, made Kinsey realize just how little sex-related research there was in the collegiate world. The lack of scientific research around humans and sexual attraction spurred him to start collecting his own data in the form of sexual histories and interviews. By 1942, he was named director of IU's Institute of Sex Research, which was backed by the Rockefeller Foundation. Kinsey created new, sometimes controversial, methods of research collection, and continued to build his library of data, which culminated in not only the *Sexual Behavior in the Human Male*, which reached number 2 on the New York Times Best Sellers List at the time, but the publishing of *Sexual Behavior in the Human Female* (1953) as well, both of which were allowed to be mailed and sold due to their medical/research basis (there was still a ban on "sexually graphic" material). Each work dove into what society deemed taboo, the private pieces of people's sexual encounters and desires, all from the perspective of science. In Kinsey's initial findings he noted that 37% of cismen (white specifically, as both books only had white participants) had a sexual encounter to orgasm with another cismale (which implies this number was most likely higher in relation to sexual experiences in general), and 16% of ciswomen actively identified as queer. He also developed what is known as the Kinsey Scale, which is scored 0 through 6, 0 being exclusively straight and 6 being exclusively gay (X for asexual) and used this scale in his book to prove that most of the US's population fell somewhere between 1 and 5. He included thousands of pieces of data and subjects and showed that sexuality is not only a vast spectrum, but that people's sexuality (and their understanding of it) changes and evolves over time. As he said, "the heterosexuality or homosexuality of many individuals is not an all-or-none proposition." In the last two years of his life, he dealt with being a victim of the red *and* lavender scares, which directly affected his health. He passed away from congestive heart failure in 1956, only three years after the release of his second famed work, but his legacy and research continued. After his death, the Institute of Sex Research was re-named the Kinsey Institute, and the study of sexology, the field he helped lay the groundwork for, became an official field of study in the Western collegiate space.

Founded somewhere around 1949, Knights of the Clock (formerly Cloistered Order of Conclaved Knights of Sophisticracy or C.L.O.C.K.S) was the first organized queer activist group that addressed the intersectional ties of queer and BIPOC equity. Though it was not the first interracial activist group (Henry Gerber's Society for Human Rights had a Black preacher named John T. Graves as its president), Knights of the Clock is the standout of Black representation in the overwhelmingly white, homophile movement. The group was founded by interracial couple Merton Bird (Bryd) and W. Dorr Legg (1904-1994) and was meant to be a mutual-aid organization whose mission it was,

> "to promote fellowship and understanding between homosexuals themselves, specifically between other races."

As for many BIPOC in America, there were (are) not only laws involving segregation, but white supremacy was embedded into our systems and structures, and this made finding housing, jobs, and surviving as a person of color, and in turn an interracial couple, extremely difficult; white privilege does not extend out, oppression creeps over. It was for these systemic issues and personal rights that Knights of the Clock rallied and for the four years it existed, it offered counseling services, housing assistance, and hosted social events to create a network for the intersectional, queer community in Los Angeles.

❧ ❧ ❧ ❧

The Knights of the Clock did not just disappear after their four-year run, in fact, quite a few of the members, including the two founders, were absorbed into the Mattachine Society (the group had had at least three names prior to that one, including Society of Fools and International Bachelors Fraternal Order for Peace and Social Dignity), which was an gay activist group secretly founded in 1950 that publicly campaigned for queer equity. The success and notability of the organization was due in part to the arrest of one of its founding members, Dale Jennings (1917-2000). On March 21, 1952, Jennings became one of the hundreds of thousands of queer people, specifically gay cismen and trans individuals, to be the victim of entrapment. The police's tactics were not merely conversations where someone agrees they are gay; in fact, judges across the country were stating that verbal confirmation of queerness was not enough to arrest someone, and individuals needed to commit "physical perversions" in order to be arrested. You may or may not be surprised at the sheer number of police officers willing to go "undercover" for these stings. **Trigger warning on assault** To show just how invasive these entrapments could be, Jennings detailed his horrific encounter, which was published in a *One Magazine* article. He explains that he was walking home through what is now MacArthur Park in Los Angeles, when a man approached and started harassing him. This person started following him home, and in fact pushed his way into

Jennings apartment:

> "I was almost relieved when he strolled into the back bedroom because now I could call the police. What I'd have said to them, I don't know and what he'd have done if he'd heard, was up to luck. Then he called twice, 'Come in here!' His voice was loud and commanding. He'd taken his jacket off, was sprawled on the bed and his shirt was unbuttoned half way down. During the tense conversation there, he asked me what kind of work I did, how much I made, and what the rent here was. Then he slapped the bed and said, 'Sit down.' Now he insisted that I was homosexual and urged me to 'let down my hair.' He'd been in the Navy and 'all us guys played around.' I told him repeatedly that he had the wrong guy; he got angrier each time I said it. At last he grabbed my hand and tried to force it down the front of his trousers. I jumped up and away. Then there was the badge, and he was snapping the handcuffs on with the remark, 'Maybe you'll talk better with my partner outside.'"

The sad truth is that this was a mild example of the entrapment that was perpetrated by police forces across the world, and it was not the special part of Jennings arrest. What made this stand out was what he did next. Jennings and the other founding members of the Mattachine Society decided to have him plead "not guilty," admit he was gay in court, and fight the charges, with a focus entirely on the legality of entrapment. They hired Syrian American George Shibley

(1910-1989), who was an all-star defense attorney known for taking up the underdog and marginalized cases, and from his opening statement there was no doubt his goal was winning. Shibley stated that his,

> "Client was admittedly homosexual, that no fine line separates the variations of sexual inclinations, and the only true pervert in the courtroom was the arresting officer."

To the shock of even Jennings himself, after forty hours of deliberation, and with eleven of the twelve jurors wanting to acquit, with one stubborn, bigoted man holding out for nothing but a guilty verdict, the case was dismissed, and Jennings was free. Even though it was barely mentioned in the newspapers, the gay telephone tree did its thing, and membership in the Mattachine Society swelled. The group would be a central part of the homophile movement for well over a decade, and though it did not make it out of the 60s (neither did the homophile movement), it gave birth, so-to-speak, to a host of other queer activist groups.

❧ ❧ ❧ ❧

Written By Family

Finding a "mainstream" book that centers around the topic of queerness? Exciting, but rare and usually written by a cis/straight-identifying person. Finding a book centered around queerness, with queer characters, by a queer person? Fieeeercccee, and not as uncommon as you think; those books are just typically less frequently discussed. As with all narratives, LGBTQIA+ stories are best told through our own voices, so here is a list that is just that, thirty books ranging from fiction to autobiography, with little blurbs and facts about each, starting all the way back in the 1800s.

1881 - *The Sins of the Cities of the Plain* by "Jack Saul" - You may notice the author's name in quotes. That is because this work was published under a pseudonym, the reason being that this is one of the earliest examples of gay erotica published in English. It is believed to be the memoir of John Saul, the same escort who was involved in quite a few queer scandals (including the Cleveland Street Scandal), so mature content warning on this salacious writing. To give you an idea of what it is about, the other title for the work is *The Recollections of a Mary-Ann, with Short Essays on Sodomy and Tribadism*. Two years after the publication there was a sequel published, *Letters from Laura and Eveline, Giving an Account of Their Mock-Marriage, Wedding Trip, etc. Published as an Appendix* *to Sins of the Cities*. Laura and Eveline referenced in the title are drag queens, or rather, potentially transwomen.

1906 - *Imre: A Memorandum* by Edward Prime-Stevenson (1858-1942) - *Imre* was originally published under the pseudonym "Xavier Mayne," which New Jersey native Prime-Stevenson used to release another queer work, *The Intersexes: A History of Similisexualism as a Problem in Social Life*, which was effectively a scholarly defense of being queer. *Imre* tells the love story of Oswald and Imre, two "insistently masculine types," who cannot seem to resist each other. A mini spoiler: what stands out about this work is that the couple remains happy in the end, which as we all know tends to be a rarity in queer romances, even now.

1928 - *The Well of Loneliness* by Radclyffe "John" Hall (1880-1943) - Preferring to be called John, Hall's *The Well of Loneliness* brought attention to lesbians', and women's ability in general, to love and find intimacy without a cis-man. Originally published in 1928, the book came under fire and was called "pornography" by the UK and US governments. In fact, the book was banned based on the official medical advice at the time that stated that it would encourage women to be lesbians and cause "a social and national disaster." Imagine, a book bringing on the lesbian revolution?! After being republished decades later, the book has been heavily debated among critics and feminist alike. It will always hold a place as a pioneering queer novel, following Stephen Gordon, a wealthy person assigned female at birth who is a "sexual invert" (the term used for gay/lesbian/transgender people of the time), who falls for Mary Llewellyn. Nothing quite explains the core of this work more powerfully than this line, "Give us also the right to our existence."

1928 - *Orlando* by Virginia Woolf (1882-1941) - *Orlando* is also from 1928, which happened to be a big year for queer literature (even more than just on this list). *Orlando* was written by Virginia Woolf (who truly lived a life that was more interesting than most fiction), as an effective love letter to her long-term girlfriend, Vita Sackville-West. The story follows Orlando, a person whose life spans over 300 years, and who lives as multiple presentations of themselves during that life, experiencing love of all genders, and expressions of all kinds. Woolf and Sackville-West love affair is chronicled in 2018's film *Vita & Virginia.*

1939 - *Diana: A Strange Autobiography* by Frances V. Rummell (1907-1969) - Given the designation of first published lesbian autobiography, *Diana* was written by Rummell under the pseudonym Diana Fredericks. Rummell, who was a teacher of French language at Stephens College, passed away before anyone ever found out that she was the author behind this landmark work. The book follows her discovering her sexuality, navigating her life, and finding love, all the things that we go through, but rarely get to see played out in a realistic, queer way.

1943 - *Our Lady of the Flowers* by Jean Genet (1910-1986) - A French novel written originally while Genet was in prison, and largely taken from his own experiences in Paris, it is not a stretch to see why the narrator of the book is in prison while telling the stories of the wonderfully camp and morose queer characters he has met in Paris. *Our Lady of the Flowers* follows Divine, a drag queen, who lives in an attic overlooking a cemetery. She resides in her home with a random cast of lovers, most notably Darling Daintyfoot. The story is fantastical, filled with love, betrayal, and murder. If you are wondering why Divine sounds familiar, it is rumored that John Waters was reading this novel when he thought to name his friend and muse, the incredible cult icon and drag legend, Divine.

1948 - *The City and the Pillar* by Gore Vidal (1925-2012) - Though it may have some problematic themes, so I give trigger warnings for assault, Vidal's third novel is significant in that it does not portray the gay character in a weak light, or end with his death or isolation from society. Following the life of Jim Willard as he discovers his attraction to men, particularly pining after his childhood friend, Bob Ford, *The City and the Pillar* is a staple in gay literature.

1952 – *The Price of Salt* by Patricia Highsmith (1921-1995) - Highsmith was already a well-known writer (in 1950 she wrote the still constantly remade, *Strangers on a Train*), when she published *Price of Salt* (later re-titled *Carol*), so it was released under the pseudonym "Claire Morgan." Besides needing to protect her career, Highsmith took many aspects of her own life, and implanted them into the story, and thus needed to protect the people who surrounded her. *The Price of Salt* follows the love story of Therese Belivet and Carol Aird, the former a twenty-something trying to launch her theater career, the latter a woman in her thirties going through a divorce. The relationship ebbs and flows, facing discrimination, and shame, and leads to finding an everlasting love.

1956 - *Giovanni's Room* by James Baldwin (1924-1987) - Baldwin is perhaps one of the greatest queer icons, as well as talents in general, to come out of the twentieth century. His way with words may still be unmatched to this day, as evident by his many quotes plastered on posters, used in activism, and as life mottos. His drive for social justice on not simply the queer but also the racial front is something by which we should all be inspired. With his second published novel, Baldwin took on the complexities of navigating gay and bisexual male relationships in society. *Giovanni's Room* contains affairs, murder, love, and self-discovery. It centers around David, an American who is contemplating marrying his girlfriend, but then falls for an Italian man named Giovanni while in Paris.

1963 - *City of the Night* by John Rechy (b. 1931) - This is the story of an unnamed "young man," a self-proclaimed hustler, as he travels across the country to various major cities, and experiences queer life, love, and dalliances (mature content warning on this one, absolutely). The novel also touches on real life queer events, one being the Cooper Do-Nuts Riot (more on this in a bit), which the author, Rechy, not only attended, but was also one of five people arrested.

1964 - *A Single Man* by Christopher Isherwood (1904-1986) - Isherwood is an author whose work most of us know but we might not realize it. In 1939, he published *Goodbye to Berlin*, a semi-autobiographical story about his time in Berlin nearing the end of the jazz age, which inspired the Broadway hit musical, *Cabaret*. His novel on this list, however, is *A Single Man*, a beautiful story that takes place over the course of one day. In the novel, we follow a day in the life of George, a professor in California, who just recently lost the love of his life and partner, Jim. We follow him as he meets a random set of people that help him rediscover what it means to live again in a new world without his love.

1971 - *Maurice* by E.M. Forster (1879-1970) - Written between 1913-1960, and finally published posthumously in 1971, Forster pulled from the real gay relationships in his life to create this novel, particularly George Merrill and his life partner, scholar and philosopher Edward Carpenter. The story follows Maurice Hall, beginning in his teen years, with his boyhood crush on Clive Durham, leading to his realization of his true nature and love, and having to choose between a love held only as a secret or a love that will travel the world with him. Summing up the beauty is a quote from *Maurice* itself, "A happy ending was imperative. I should not have bothered to write otherwise. I was determined that in fiction anyway two men should fall in love and remain in it for the ever and ever that fiction allows."

1973 - *Rubyfruit Jungle* by Rita Mae Brown (b. 1944) - This was the first novel for Brown and was based on her own sexual awakening. The novel, which is named after the slang term in the story for vagina, describes the coming-of-age and sexuality of Molly Bolt. It so openly shares her first experiences with a girl, her rocky relationship with her mother, and her journey to just exist and be herself.

1978 - *Tales of the City* by Armistead Maupin (b. 1944) - Not to be confused with the overarching series, *Tales of the City* was the work that sparked it all. Originally released in weekly installments in the *San Francisco Chronicle*, *Tales of the City* and its subsequent novels have been adapted into TV shows (a Netflix series starring Elliot Page being one), musicals, and even radio shows. It chronicles the realities of the queer characters that live in the apartments at 28 Barbary Lane in San Francisco.

1981 - *The Celluloid Closet* by Vito Russo (1946-1990) - Arguably one of the most important reference works when it comes to Hollywood's portrayal and treatment of queer people over the last century and written by one of the co-founders of GLAAD (Gay and Lesbian Alliance Against Defamation), *The Celluloid Closet* is a must-read of queer history. Russo's book was even made into a documentary, featuring a host of incredible names; unfortunately, he was unable to see its release, as he had passed away five years prior. *The Celluloid Closet* is extensively researched, detailing how queer lives were hidden and often silenced, particularly with the implementation of the Hays Code. If you ever wonder or want more understanding as to why it is so important for queer voices to tell our own stories and be represented in the media, this is a wonderful historical background. There is also a fascinating documentary about Russo's life and life's work entitled, *Vito* (2011).

1982 - *Zami: A New Spelling of My Name* by Audre Lorde (1934-1992) - Powerful and raw, as is much of Lorde's work, *Zami* is a biomythography, a genre that was created by this book, which is part biography, part history and part myth. *Zami* tells Lorde's story from childhood through adulthood, never shying away from the real issues she faced from racism to classism, while also showing the joys of new love and relationships. Lorde was the state poet laureate of New York, and self-described "Black, lesbian, mother, warrior, poet," and all those titles can be found in this breathtaking work.

1993 - *Stone Butch Blues* by Leslie Feinberg (1949-2014) - A deeply meaningful look at the multifaceted identity of humans. We follow the main character Jesse Goldberg, who faces antisemitism, classism, homophobia, and transphobia, among other things, while navigating life in 1970s America. Feinberg mirrored much of hir life in the storyline of Goldberg, from the evolution of Goldberg's gender expression to hir political activism and union organizing.

1994 - *Notes of a Crocodile* by Qiu Miaojin (1969-1995) - Told from the perspective of Lazi, a lesbian university student in Taiwan, the book follows her ups and downs as she falls for an older woman and gets advice and support from an eclectic band of queer friends. *Notes of a Crocodile* is considered a cult classic, not simply for the novel's so-honestly-lesbian take on the world, but for Miaojin herself. She wrote this novel at just twenty-five years old, and it was published only months before she died by suicide while in Paris earning her degree. In her short life, Miaojin was able to leave a legacy, and transform lesbian literature as we know it.

1999 - *Party Monster* by James St. James (b. 1966) - This is the story of true events of the Club Kid scene in New York. Club Kids were the Kardashians of the 90s, with the whole murder plot line sprinkled in. In the case of the Club Kids, however, it was the end to the story and not the beginning. St. James tells the story of the rise and fall of the Club Kids in NYC, both due to one central person,

Michael Alig. Through St. James' firsthand accounts of the parties, sex, drugs, outfits, and shock, you get a glimpse into what this little corner of NYC's gay 90s underground scene was like, and see where gay icons like Amanda Lepore and Leigh Bowery found their first fifteen minutes of fame.

1999 - *Exile and Pride: Disability, Queerness, and Liberation* by Eli Clare - In *Exile and Pride*, Clare goes beyond simply queer existence to share his story and life of intersectionality as a white, genderqueer, disabled activist. A foundation for so much of the

discussions about disability politics and queerness, Clare so transparently examines how our understanding of ourselves is constantly changing and has evolved over time. He is direct in his examination of the world from capitalism to ableism, to the need for equity in access, true and real accessibility for everyone. This is very much a lesson in understanding and education in reflection, wrapped in an autobiography.

2006 - *Fun Home: A Family Tragicomic* by Alison Bechdel (b. 1960) - Animation is a great way to bluntly speak about topics that society deems "sensitive", and *Fun Home* is no exception to that notion. This comic memoir, that took seven years to create, gives us a look inside Bechdel's youth, dealing with gender, sexuality, abuse, suicide, and dysfunctional family life. It is real, and relatable, and not done in your typical linear comic fashion. This seven-year labor is just one of a host of works that Bechdel has provided the world. Another reason you might know her is the Bechdel Test. The Bechdel Test, in its most basic form, is meant to measure representation of women in fiction/entertainment; it is simple in that, to pass the test, a work needs to feature at least two female characters, who have names, and who talk to each other about something other than a man. If you think that sounds simple, statistically, 50% of all Academy Award nominees would not pass the test.

2015 - *Under the Udala Trees* by Chinelo Okparanta (b. 1981) - Nigerian American Okparanta gives us this stunning lesbian story set against the backdrop of 1960s war-torn Nigeria. The book's journey follows Ijeoma as she deals with war, loss, religion, oppression, and ultimately love. *Under the Udala Trees* gives an authentic take on the intersectional battle so many face—culture vs. sexuality—and how, in one novel, a woman handles and processes it all to come out stronger in the end.

2017 - *Trap Door: Trans Cultural Production and the Politics of Visibility* by Johanna Burton, Reina Gosset & Eric Stanley - Essays, art, history, and all of it centered around trans existence and place in society, *Trap Door* is saturated with information that is so often overlooked. Analyzing the paradox that is the rise and appearing "acceptance" of trans people, coupled with the increasing hatred and violence against the community. This work is meant to make you take a step back, and then get ready to stampede forward toward change.

2018 - *Bingo Love* by Tee Franklin - Franklin, who is an activist and writer, is a pioneer in her own right, being the first Black, queer, disabled woman to write for DC Comics *Harley Quinn* comic series. To make that accomplishment even more badass, the story she wrote centers around Harley Quinn and Poison Ivy's lesbian love affair. With *Bingo Love*, Franklin created a love story that is often omitted, that of not only bisexuals, but also bisexual women of color. A graphic novella that absorbs you into the love story of Mari and Hazel, beginning in 1963 and following the course of their lives over the next sixty years. We watch as they live their separate lives, marry men, have children, but somehow cross paths in the end. This is a bit of a tearjerker, but worth every second of it.

2018 - *Little Fish* by Casey Plett (b. 1987) - A novel wrapped in mystery, trauma, authenticity, and history, *Little Fish* delves into something that is rather common, looking at our bloodlines to figure out our queer past. We watch Wendy, a woman who is trans, begin to realize that her grandfather was most likely trans too, all while dealing with a host of issues from suicide to alcoholism. Plett won a Lambda Literary Award for this novel, and it is no surprise why.

2019 - *Space Between: Explorations of Love, Sex, and Fluidity* by Nico Tortorella (b. 1988) - You might know this author's name (they are the tattoo covered love interest from *Younger)* but what you might not know about them is their incredible aptitude for writing. Following up on their poetry collection *All of it is You*, Tortorella's memoir *Space Between* further builds on their motto that everything, all of it, even the space between, is us. In their own voice, Tortorella tells us their story through addiction, fame, and self-destruction, and how it all led to them exploring and finding their authentic self. It was in this exploration of fluidity of self, from gender expression to relationships, that Tortorella was able to find balance, growth, and ultimately peace in their ever-evolving journey of life.

2019 - *On Earth We're Briefly Gorgeous* by Ocean Vuong (b. 1988) - Somewhat mirroring his own life, Vuong's debut novel, which is written as a letter, is beautifully tragic. The writer of the letter is Little Dog, a gay Vietnamese American man, who tells not only his story, but also those of his mother and grandmother. Giving us a look into the civilian victims of war, particularly the long-term effects, and how that trauma is handed down, Vuong delivers a heart achingly stunning work.

2020 - *Here for It: How to Save Your Soul in America* by R. Eric Thomas - A hilarious, and honest take on code switching and the intersectionality of his identity, Thomas brings us through his life, with all the ups, downs, and awkward moments in between. Explaining the moments in his life that he was basically informed he was different, and how that shaped who he is today, *Here for It* tells one person's story of navigating society, and how his identity as a gay Black man fits in it all.

2021 - *Obie is Man Enough* by Schuyler Bailar (b. 1996) - This is a young adult novel that every age should read. Written by the first ever trans D1 NCAA male athlete (Harvard alumnus), *Obie is Man Enough* submerges us into the title character's (Obie) life as a tween swimming phenom, who happens to be transgender. We get to see his experiences of starting on a new team, having his first crush, dealing with bullies, and striving to be a success in a world where sometimes he feels like an outsider. Besides centering around a trans male character, which is a rarity, Bailar's debut novel shows us a fully realized character. In Bailar's own words on his work,

> "I wrote this book to share a story about a transgender kid that isn't solely focused on his transness. I want kids and everyone to see that we exist in our entirety."

2021 - *Greedy: Notes from a Bisexual Who Wants Too Much* by Jen Winston - Have you ever been called greedy simply because you are willing to admit you can be attracted to more than one type of person? Winston has, and that is sadly something they have in common with many bisexual people. In this hilarious memoir written in essays, Winston takes us on her journey of self, all the ebbs, flows, realizations and un-realizations and explains how society, stereotypes, microagressions and education have shaped and led them to be the bisexual, comedic genius that tweets before us.

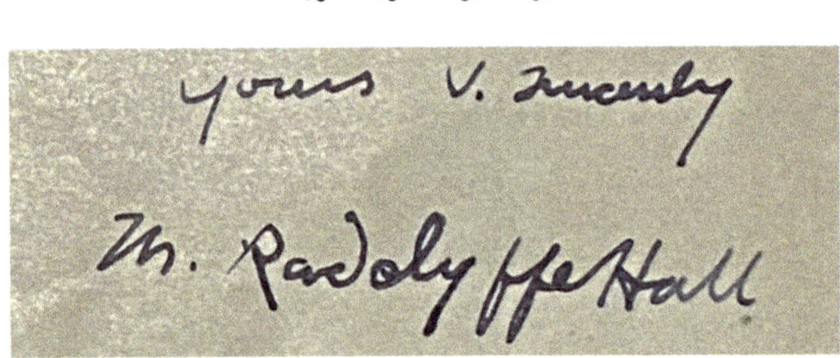

Radclyffe Hall autograph, 1930

Twelve years after Gloria's in NYC was defeated in their argument that LGBTQIA+ people simply existing in a space was not illegal, in 1951, the Black Cat Café in San Francisco was able to use that defense and win. The Black Cat was owned by Sol Stoumen (1911-1987), an ally who escaped Austria during WWII and purchased the bar in 1945. It was considered the epitome of San Franciscan bohemian life during the 1940s and 50s, and was frequented by names like John Steinbeck, Bette Davis, and queer icon Tallulah Bankhead. It was also the place that launched the career of José Sarria (1922-2013), the first openly gay person to run of political office (in 1961), and though he lost, he set in motion the visible power of what can happen when LGBTQIA+ people come together. The Black Cat was truly a place for everyone, as one patron listed in the documentary *Word is Out* (1977), there were sailors, sex workers, painters, drag queens, and straight couples, to name a few; everyone and anyone was welcomed. This openly queer environment drew the ire of the local police department as well as the military police (it was a banned bar for the sailors stationed in San Fran). For over two years, the Black Cat was harassed and infiltrated by the police as they documented the patrons' actions and attempted to entrap them. After a few dozen raids and arrests associated with the bar, its liquor license was revoked, but instead of simply turning away the queer patrons to get it back, Stoumen decided to sue the government. In 1951, his case made it all the way to the California Supreme Court, and he argued that the mere existence of LGBTQIA+ people in the establishment did not constitute "immoral" acts and that the police provided no evidence of "sexual perversion." The court agreed with Stoumen, the prosecution supplied no concrete evidence, and the license would be reinstated. Though this was a win, it set in motion a few things: firstly, the police now had a vendetta against the Black Cat; secondly it established that the police would now attempt to meticulously document queer acts; thirdly, though it meant that gay people could exist in a space together, any physical contact would be deemed evidence of "immoral acts"; and finally, California established the Department of Alcoholic Beverage Control and gave it the ability to close down places that were considered "resorts" for queer people, which it did with homophobic vigor. Any bar that allowed its patrons to be visibly queer would be shut down, so bars would encourage their guest to use restrooms, or backrooms, so as to not be seen in the common areas. These private areas are what protected the bars from police observations, and usually gave the establishments enough cover to stay open. There were certain bars that became very good at this, and those were most often the targets of the longer sting operations. Mary's First and Last Chance Bar in Oakland was one such bar, having a nine-month-long waste of taxpayer dollars. In 1959, Mary's decided to follow in Stoumen's footsteps, and not only openly admitted in court that the bar was opened as a queer bar, but also said they were not going to stop serving their community. Mary's case (Vallerga v. Department of Alcoholic Beverage Control) was an example of the LGBTQIA+ community's ability not only to communicate in code, but also to be hyper aware of our surroundings, and thus safety, which in turn led to the police having little evidence. The only semi-clear example of queerness they could provide in their nine-month investigation was the following,

"Helen Davis, a policewoman, was on the premises in May 1956 with another policewoman, Marge Gwinn. Buddy, a

> female waitress, greeted the policewomen who were later joined by the lesbian, Shirleen. Shirleen told Marge, 'you're a cute little butch.' Shirleen later grabbed Marge and kissed her."

Besides the fact that this just seems like Marge may have been the queerest person in the group, when this case made its way to the California Supreme Court, they ruled that not only was there not enough evidence provided, but the fact that the police just chose to watch over and over and not notify the owners of the establishment negates their whole ability to hold the bars liable for queer people existing in their space. Again, this was absolutely a win, but bigotry will always find loopholes, and that came in the form of laws around clothing presentation and the physical intimacy and private lives of LGBTQIA+ people.

❧ ❧ ☙ ☙

Niche magazines became more and more popular through the first half of the twentieth century, but there was a gap in the gay interest market, and this was due to both society and legal system bias. In order to be publicly distributed, books, magazines, and even plays had to be queer coded, so in 1951, Bob Mizer (1922-1992) created *Physique Pictorial*, a physical "fitness" focused magazine that displayed scantily clad, muscular male models and sparked the "physique" or "beefcake" era. Mizer began his photography career in the early 1940s under the tutorship of Frederick Kovert (1901-1949), a silent film drag queen star. In 1945, Mizer opened

Athletic Model Guild (AMG), which was both a modeling agency and a place where he would photograph subjects himself. The clearly gay messaging of his photographs, as well as rumors of his models' also being sex workers, drew the attention of the local Los Angeles police, and Mizer was arrested multiple times on charges ranging from obscenity violations to running an escorting ring. The police harassment did not deter him from his art, and he continued to photograph, and took his work to the next level with the inception of *Physique Pictorial*. By covering the gay intent of the magazine with the body building facade, Mizer was able to (barely) skate by the Comstock laws banning "obscene" items from being mailed. Each quarterly issue featured photos of different models from AMG, usually in some costume or sport pose, with articles about them and their routines, and the option to purchase individual photos. The publication ran from 1951-1990, and besides inspiring countless other photographers like Bruce of LA (Bruce Bellas, 1909–1974) and Robert Mapplethorpe (1946-1989), the magazine was also the springboard for artists like Tom of Finland (Touko Valio Laaksonen, 1920-1991), George Quaintance (1902-1957) and Etienne (Dom Orejudos, 1933-1991).

Born in Newark, NJ in 1952, Tracey "Africa" Norman most certainly dreamed of a glamorous life but had no idea that she would be photographed for Italian *Vogue* and *Essence*, have a contract with Avon skincare, be a model for the Balenciaga showroom in Paris, and at twenty-three would be the face on the Clairol "Born Beautiful" color No. 512, Dark Auburn. All these feats would be incredible on their own, but to add some intersectional layers to this icon of a human, Norman is the first known transwoman to accomplish any of these things. She began her authentic journey on her graduation day in 1969, where she honestly told her mom exactly who she was, and in true parental fashion, her mother hugged her, said she had always known, and continued on. A few years later, in one of those serendipitous moments, Norman exited a subway in NYC and saw a group of models that she idolized. Knowing that there were shows happening, she decided to follow them, slipping in behind then at the casting call. She went into the auditions and her charm and beauty had her a professional modeling job the next day. For a little over half a decade she traveled the world and was able to live all her dreams, until she was outed by a person on set who recognized her from high school. From there she was cruelly ostracized from the fashion world but was able to find a home in the drag world. She became a member of the House of Africa, where she flourished amongst people who understood her on the most foundational level. She was inducted into the Ballroom Hall of Fame (drag ballroom) in 2001 and continues to live her most iconic life.

Around the middle of the twentieth century, the United States government decided to overhaul its extremely racist quota immigration policy and replace it with the no-quota, still racist Immigration and Nationality Act of 1952 (INA), but the catch was they added a line about queer people. Directly due to the ongoing lavender scare, the US government sought to ban queer people from being able to become American citizens. While creating the INA, legislators wanted to include the word "homosexual," but the Public Health Service (PHS), suggested that since queerness is *difficult to diagnose*, that they use more general terms that could cover LGBTQIA+ people, and so they went with a ban on "aliens afflicted with a psychopathic personality, epilepsy or a mental defect." As well as making sure that their intent was clear, with this asterisk, "[t]his change of nomenclature is not to be construed in any way as modifying the intent to exclude all aliens who are sexual deviates." Under this law, any person coming into the US could (and would) be interrogated by immigration services about their sexual experiences and desires, and if deemed potentially queer (usually based on stereotypes) they would be sent to PHS to be examined and "diagnosed." Even six years after "homosexuality" (as it was listed by the American Psychiatric Association, APA) was removed from the DSM (Diagnostic and Statistical Manual of Mental Disorders), Asst. Attorney General John M. Harmon upheld the ban, stating in 1979 he was still, "statutorily required to enforce the exclusion of homosexual aliens," which with all things considered makes utterly no sense since the law did not ban gay people specifically. With no more false medical backing, the true homophobic motives shine through. This version of the INA stayed on US law books until 1990 and made the United States the only nation that had a ban on queer people entering the country.

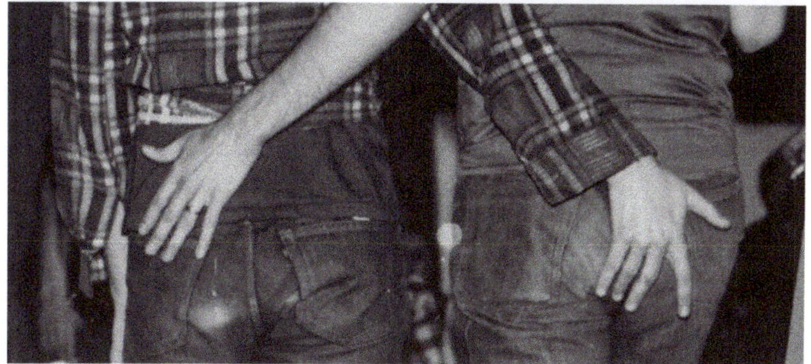

One of the driving forces in the APA's removing "homosexuality" from the DSM was the research of psychologist and UCLA professor, Evelyn Hooker PhD (1907-1996), which she was inspired to undertake due to a budding friendship with her gay student, Sam From (c.1925-1956). Hooker grew up in a low-income household, and the one thing that was always instilled in her was that an education was the one thing that would always be her own, so school is where she found her success. She obtained a scholarship to the University of Colorado, where she received her undergraduate and master's degrees, and then she became one of the only women to graduate from the PhD program in experimental psychology at Johns Hopkins University in 1932. By 1937, Hooker already had years of teaching under her belt, and was living in Berlin after receiving a fellowship to study at the Berlin Psychoanalytic Institute. It was here, after witnessing the horrors of the Holocaust and WWII firsthand, that she began to truly delve into applying her background in science to help solve social injustices. After returning to the US, she began working at UCLA where she met From in 1944. From confided in her that he was gay and urged her to study his friends and him, to prove that being queer was not an illness, and Hooker agreed. Over the next few years, they became close friends, and Hooker became one of the only straight people to be welcomed without hesitation into the gay subculture of Los Angeles. She met with people like Christopher Isherwood (the one who inspired *Cabaret*), who happened to be a close friend of From's, and became immersed in the world that is queerness. Hooker decided to take her research to the next level and controversially applied for a grant with the National Institute of Mental Health (NIMH) in 1953. She proposed a psychological study comparing gay and straight cismen. She was awarded the grant and began her research of thirty gay cismen and thirty straight cismen using three standardized phycological exams that science at the time believed could determine someone's sexuality: Rorschach (inkblot test), MAPS test (Make-a-Picture-Story, arranging photos to tell a story), and TATS (Thematic apperception test, where the subject is shown a picture and must make up a story). After the subjects completed the exams, Hooker then had three experts, who all swore they could pick the gay men out in a heartbeat, review the findings. No one should be surprised that none of the experts, nor anyone else who reviewed the findings, could tell the difference between the two groups. What her research proved was that there was no connection between queerness and psychological maladjustment, which was the "reasoning" used in many anti-LGBTQIA+ stances. After three years of research and further evidence, in 1956, Hooker presented her findings to the APA's annual convention in Chicago and immediately shifted the psychological view on gay people. She said that presentation was one of the best days of her life, and that research garnered her APA's Distinguished Contribution to

Psychology in the Public Interest award in 1992. In her acceptance speech she said she was sharing the award with the LGBTQIA+ community and spoke on the importance of her research both to her personally and to the world. She chose to end her speech with a line from a letter a gay man had sent her, "I think you did it because you knew what love was when you saw it, and you knew that gay love was like all other love."

Throughout time, people have blamed everything but the patriarchy and white supremacy for issues in the world. For instance, when it comes to failing schools and crime among children, video games are a nice scapegoat, and prior to that, it was comic books. In 1954, Dr. Fredric Wertham (1895-1981) released the dramatically named, *Seduction of the Innocent*, which basically held comic books, and not family units/education systems/government programs, responsible for the "corruption" of children. Wertham's issues with comic books ranged from the violence and crime depicted, to the overt gay relationships that were seen in series like *Batman*, and Congress took notice. The same year he published his book, Wertham spoke to the Senate Subcommittee on Juvenile Delinquency and the comic book industry was effectively put on notice. The industry formed the Comics Code Authority, which was like the Hays Code and had similar results. The code outlined what was acceptable for comic books, and their rules covered things like what types of crimes could and could not appear and how the superhero outfits would look. It completely banned any reference to drugs or magic that involved the devil, and when it came to queerness it had two main rules, "The treatment of love-romance stories shall emphasize the value of home and the sanctity of marriage," and "sex perversion or any inference to same is strictly forbidden." The result of these rules was more than just erasing gay stories from comics for the next thirty-five years (the code lasted until 1989); what it actually did was further codified queer coding into the Western mainstream. Queer coding, and in turn queerbaiting, in entertainment is essentially the use of LGBTQIA+ stereotypes to allude to a character's identity without ever actually saying it (i.e. making a cismale character appear more effeminate, depicting bonded relationships between people who identify as the same gender), and it is sometimes used to bait queer and ally audiences in, and other times is used to negatively tie queerness with what society would deem "bad." The latter is what both codes (Comic and Hays) chose to do with their queer characters, to further entwine cis/het society's view of queerness with villainy, and that is quite literal. In comic books, this notion of immediate negative thought in reference to queerness was being pushed to children. The villains became more queer, with bad guys like the Flame-Master, Rainbow Raider, Dr. X/Double X, and The Shade showing up, and their outfits were more theatrical, we'll say. Examples of the villain having queer-coded behavior, voice, or mannerisms can be seen, well, pretty much everywhere in tv and film: Governor Ratcliffe from *Pocahontas* dresses like Liberace, Ursula was literally drawn to look like Divine, Team Rocket from *Pokémon*…no more needs to be said on that one, Scar is the unmarried bachelor uncle who has tons of wrist flips, Maleficent is an independent woman who does not need a man, like ever, Captain Hook is a sea queen who lived with his partner Smee, Shego is a lesbian feminist icon, and Jafar oozes gay sass and his power is held in a phallic staff, to name a few. These are only a small fraction of the examples that could have been used, and are only in the realm of children's entertainment, not film and tv in its entirety. The next time you feel yourself rooting for the "villain" or finding that the evil queen is actually *your* queen/icon/diva, maybe it is because that is the character that is meant to be most like you. (As a note on fabulous villain icons, in the live action *Kim Possible*, Shego was played, rightfully so, by queer actor Taylor Ortega)

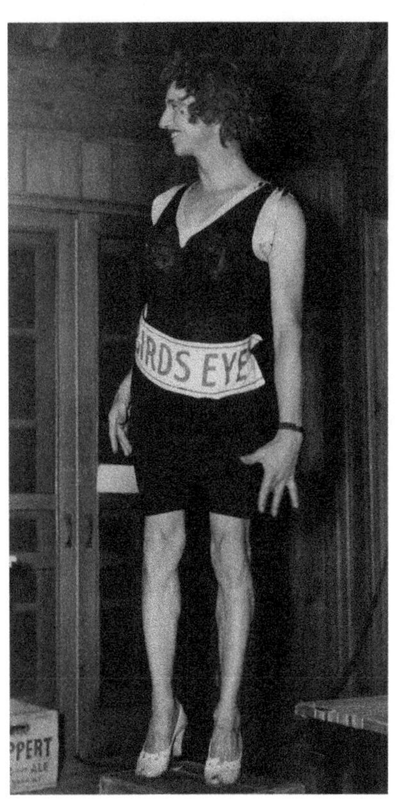

"Would you like to be a part of the group of six of us that are putting together a secret society for lesbians?" That was the question that Rose Bamberger, a factory-working Filipino American who just wanted to dance with her girlfriend, posed to Del Martin (1921-2008) and Phyllis Lyon (1924-2020) in 1955. Though the question seems as mundane as a secret society can sound, this conversation sparked the founding of the Daughters of Bilitis (DOB), which was the first "official" lesbian organization in the United States (to note, it was founded by Bamberger, an immigrant, who was a woman of color). The conversation started because the couples did not have a place to simply be themselves and dance (dancing for couples of the same gender identity was illegal at the time), and in turn found it difficult to meet friends. As is the theme of being queer in the cis/het world, the DOB picked their name as a nod to lesbianism, but one that was so coded that it was queer enough that other LGBTQIA+ people would know, but not so queer that cis/het people would be aware. Bilitis was taken from the poem *The Songs of Bilitis* (1894) by French poet Pierre Louÿs (1870-1925), which was meant to mimic the OG lesbian poet, Sappho, in its writing and is considered a lesbian cult classic. So, it was the perfect moniker for the newly formed group. There were a lot of changes and growth for the DOB very quickly, and the shift to being more visible caused a few of the original members to step away from the group for fear of being institutionalized, thrown in jail, or deported (these consequences highlight the issue with white centering of intersectional issues). Within the first year, the DOB went from small "Gab 'n' Javas," (their name for their living room discussions) to publishing the first nationally distributed lesbian journal, entitled *The Ladder*, which acted as a go-to for advice, book reviews, poems, news, art, and more for the lesbian community. By January 1957, DOB had opened a shared office with the Mattachine Society at 693 Mission St. in San Francisco, and by the following year they were stirring up enough good trouble to be under the watch of the local police, as well as the FBI. The DOB focused on creating a community that fostered self-acceptance first, which Martin, the organization's first president, stated was core to being able to advocate for one's rights. In 1960, after creating chapters in almost every major city in the US, the DOB held their first national convention at the Hotel Whitcomb in San Francisco. The topic was "A Look at the Lesbian," and it had panels, keynotes, a banquet, and a lunch, which was interrupted by the SFPD. The police showed up planning to arrest any banquet attendee who was wearing clothing that was not tied to their sex assigned at birth, but the DOB was a homophile group centered around conformity, and every person at the event was dressed accordingly, so the police had no one to take in. Some of the speakers at the event included guests who were homophobic, and the intention in inviting them was to open a dialogue of sorts, around queer rights. The conversations went about as well as one would imagine. One speaker was Sidney Feinberg, the North Coastal Area Administrator of the California Department of Alcoholic Beverage Control, who was there to defend the ABC's practice of harassing and closing gay bars. When the crowd started demanding answers, Fienberg began getting flustered, and according to Helen Sandoz (1920-1987) in one of her *Ladder* articles,

> "Another queried, "Sir, would it be considered 'indecent' in a bar for men to be dancing together?" Mr. Feinberg opined that it would. The young man asked, "Why?" Mr. Feinberg said that such a thing was offensive. Another male member of the audience asked rather curtly, "Offensive to whom?" Mr. Feinberg became even more agitated, and the tension in the audience rose proportionately. "Offensive to the public." Someone else asked, "Who decides what is offensive to the public? You?"

The DOB continued holding these conferences biennially and printing *The Ladder* monthly, over the next decade, continuing to foster open conversations around queerness and creating a national network of lesbians, which helped lay the groundwork for the next stage of the queer revolution.

❧ ❧ ❧ ❧

After multiple magazines, including *Esquire*, rejected his short story, entitled *The Crooked Man*, which was about a future world in which straight people are treated as queer people are, Charles

Beaumont (1929-1967) found a place to share his work when Hugh Hefner (1926-2017) decided to publish it in the August 1955 edition of *Playboy*. Beaumont, who would go on to write more than twenty episodes of *The Twilight Zone*, had written *The Crooked Man* as a commentary on the horrendous treatment of queer people in modern society. *Spoiler alert, but it will still be worth the read* The story follows Jesse, a cisman who is in love with a ciswoman named Mina, but in the current Big Brother-esque world, being straight means losing your job, going to prison, and getting "the Cure," which is comparable to conversion therapy, just the conversion here would be converting *to* being gay. In Beaumont's work the political official that was the catalyst, Senator Knudson, makes a statement on straight people that sounds terrible, and is only made more appalling when you realize these things were *actually* said about queer people,

> "The disease that throws men and women, together in this dreadful abnormal relationship and leads to acts of retrogression–retrogression that will, unless it is stopped and stopped fast, push us inevitably back to the status of animals–this is to be considered as any other disease. It must be conquered as heart trouble, cancer, polio."

Prior to Knudson, being straight was "immoral and perverted," but it was not illegal, but now all straight behavior is completely underground, and straight people are constantly worried about being arrested. Jesse's thoughts run rampant with fear that someone in the bar will know that he is straight. When Jesse finally gets to be with Mina, it is short lived because the vice squad has been watching them the entire time. The story's heartbreaking end comes as Jesse and Mina are being pulled away to be sent to get "the Cure," and Jesse realizes that he was going to lose Mina no matter what,

> "Then he knew. He knew what she had come to tell him tonight: that even if they hadn't been caught–she would have submitted to the Cure voluntarily. No more worries then, no more guilt. No more meeting at midnight dives, feeling shame, feeling dirt."

To no one's surprise, the *Playboy* audience missed the larger point, and wrote in to complain about the nature and concept of Beaumont's work. Hefner wanted to make sure the meaning of the story was clear, as well as the stance of his magazine, so he released this to-the-point response to the grievances, "If it was wrong to persecute heterosexuals in a homosexual society, then the reverse was wrong, too."

❧ ❧ ❧ ❧

Grey's Anatomy was not too far off in having Arizona be a lesbian, because when it comes to American pediatrics the leading power couple will always be Ethel Collins Dunham (1883–1969) and Martha May Eliot (1891-1978). Dunham and Eliot began their almost sixty-year relationship when they met as undergrads at Bryn

Mawr College and started their parallel lives in medicine. After graduating, the pair entered medical school at Johns Hopkins University, where they were considered top of their class, which got them noticed by other institutions. By 1921, they were the first two female professors at Yale's School of Medicine, a school they remained with for almost thirty years, until leaving to work with the World Health Organization (WHO) in Geneva (where Eliot is the only woman to have signed the WHO Constitution). If all of those were not enough accomplishments, Dunham was appointed head of the American Pediatric Society' (APS) Neonatal studies in 1933 based on her extensive, and almost unheard of, research on premature birth care. Eliot is also credited with helping care for over 1,500,000 babies by establishing appropriate care for military birthing spouses during WWII, as well as helping discover the cure for rickets. A final accomplishment (but certainly not all of them), Dunham and Eliot were the first and second ciswomen to receive the John Howland Award, which is the APS highest honor, which they received in 1957 and 1967, respectively. Over the course of their fifty-nine-year relationship the couple rarely spent time apart, but when they did for the odd research project here and there, they sent love letters back and forth. Even five decades in, they would still miss each other, as Eliot said sweetly in one of their letters, "How I count the time until you do arrive. I miss you my darling."

When the Supreme Court issued its decision on One, Inc. v. Olesen, on January 13, 1958, it was done without hearing any arguments or briefs, and it was only one simple sentence, "The petition for writ of certiorari is granted and the judgment of the United States Court of Appeals for the Ninth Circuit is reversed." There was no fanfare, no opinions of the court listed, no list of the 5-4 voting breakdown, but what it was to Eric Julber (b.1925), the lawyer who worked pro bono for four years, and to One Inc., the gay activist group that was an offshoot of the Mattachine Society, was an unimaginable victory. It started in 1953, when One, the year-old homophile group, had their first run in with the Los Angeles Postmaster. In January of that year, One had begun publishing *One* magazine, which was billed as the "The Homosexual Magazine," and had articles from queer political issues to LGBTQIA+ short stories and poems. As mentioned, the Comstock laws of 1873 decreed things deemed "obscene" could not be sent through the United States Post Office, and so the LA Postmaster tried holding the magazine in August of 1953. The group was able to finagle their way out of that situation, but they only bought themselves a year, because on October 20,1954 they were notified that all copies of their October issue would be held at the post office indefinitely. One held a board meeting where they asked their counsel, Julber, who was a newly confirmed straight lawyer with a passion for civil liberty cases, what they should do; his opinion was fight. The government noted two stories from the October issue that they said made the work "obscene," those were a lesbian story titled "Sappho Remembered," by James Barr, pen name Jane Dahr, and gay poem, "Lord Samuel and Lord Montagu," submitted by an anonymous author. The two works, which made up a collective six pages of the entire magazine, were apparently too much for Postmaster Otto K. Olesen, and so the entire work was deemed obscene. Not a group to be stopped by one bump, One continued, even publishing an article about how there were still gay FBI agents and queer people were perfectly capable of serving their country, after which the FBI began to investigate the organization itself. The Associate Director at the time, Clyde Tolson even said, "I think we should take on this crowd and make them 'put up or shut up.'" Julber filed his first motion on behalf of One in 1955, by himself, after being denied assistance from the ACLU and numerous other organizations. In his case he argued that there was nothing obscene about the work at all, because queer people have aspirations, relationships, and issues just like anyone else, and deserve a space within which they can discuss them. When the case was finally heard in 1956, Julber and One lost their argument, they appealed and lost again in 1957, and the next step was the Supreme Court. Julber took a different route and went to Washington DC, not to meet with the Justices but to see their court clerks. He knew the influence the clerks had on court decisions and decided to plant the seeds, so he brought with him a stack of copies of *One* magazine. He gave the copies to the clerks and told them about the case, hoping the Supreme Court would eventually hear arguments on it. His plan worked, just not the way he thought. The clerks did write research in favor of One, but Julber would never stand before the court to argue the case. Behind the scenes the research was being done and one clerk even wrote, "there is no doubt in my mind that" the lower courts "applied a different standard to this magazine than it would have to a magazine portraying sexual relations between males and females." Four months after Julber traveled to DC, he received a letter in the mail telling him not only had the Supreme

Court taken his case, but also, he had won. Though the decision did not state it, what the victory meant was that a work being queer in nature did not innately make it obscene, and it validated queer writing as being protected under the First Amendment, as well as holding social importance.

When *A Raisin in the Sun* premiered in 1959, it became the first play written by a Black woman to be produced on Broadway and is considered one of the greatest plays of all time. The "young, gifted and Black" writer who wrote it was Lorraine Hansberry (1930-1965), and she identified as a "heterosexually married lesbian." Her award-winning work took on the still very real story of a Black family dealing with systemic racism, while simply trying to provide for themselves. James Baldwin summed up the massive importance of this work when he said, "never before, in the entire history of the American theater, had so much of the truth of Black people's lives been seen on the stage." Perhaps one of the aspects that truly made this work so meaningful is that Hansberry based the play on her own family's battles with the racist housing policies and neighbors in Chicago. When she was eight years old her father bought a house in a predominantly white neighborhood, and almost immediately her family was dealing with racist mobs, threats of violence, and a lawsuit that made it all the way to the Supreme Court; and in this way, Hansberry's life was thrust into activism. After moving to Harlem in 1951, she began writing for *Freedom* and working with names like W.E.B Du Bois (1868-1963) and Langston Hughes. She was a vocal advocate for the civil rights movement, calling out (accurately) how white supremacy was ingrained in our systems of government. This point gained the attention of the FBI. Besides civil rights, Hansberry was passionate about gender equality, and on the more private side, LGBTQIA+ rights. She wrote articles for *The Ladder* and *One Magazine* (previously mentioned lesbian/gay magazines) where she wrote queer stories, talked about liberation, and shared bits of her personal life and lesbian identity. Her life was cut short at thirty-four by pancreatic cancer, but the world was given a few more works, one being an autobiography of sorts entitled, *To Be Young, Gifted and Black.* Her ex-husband, whom she kept a friendship with after their divorce, compiled interviews, letters, journal entries, and unpublished lines and turned Hansberry's life, described and written in her own words, into a play and later a book. Hansberry created a legacy of art in her life and has inspired countless creators since her passing, most notably is Nina Simone's hit song "To Be Young, Gifted and Black," which was written in memory of Hansberry and has been covered by icons like Aretha Franklin and Elton John.

❧ ❧ ☙ ☙

Stonewall was not the first riot by LGBTQIA+ people against police brutality and abuse of queer people in society, in fact, there were a considerable number of events prior to that fateful June 1969 event. One occurred ten years before, in 1959, when transwomen and sex workers rose up and fought back at the Cooper Do-nuts Riot in Los Angeles. Cooper Do-nuts was a twenty-four-hour coffee shop that was located right near a few gay clubs and became a home to the gender diverse community that was often excluded from the gay

scene due to transphobia and police harassment ("cross-dressing" laws were the target for police). One May night, two police officers came into Cooper's checking IDs to validate the clothing that people were wearing, and to arrest those they deemed in the wrong attire. The officers attempted to arrest five people, including transwomen, sex workers, and John Rechy (the aforementioned author of *City of the Night*), but on this night the patrons of Cooper's were done. As the police tried shoving the arrestees into the squad car, the people of Cooper's emptied into the streets and began throwing coffee cups, donuts, and anything at their disposal, at the officers. The onslaught of garbage was enough to cause the officers to release the five patrons and drive off with no arrests for the night. Another pre-Stonewall riot happened in the Tenderloin district of San Francisco, at Compton's Cafeteria. Compton's, like Cooper's, was a safe haven for trans and gender-diverse people, and so it was the target of constant police attacks. In August 1966, the police entered Compton's and tried arresting a transwoman, who had no time for that nonsense and proceeded to throw a coffee in the cop's face. In this action, all the patrons of Compton's decided to act, and they began to riot. Windows were shattered, high heels were thrown, newsstands were burned, and the queer, mainly transgender, people of the Tenderloin put their foot down on being harassed. These events, though often overlooked in history, were some of the first documented uprisings of queer people in the US against the institution of law enforcement, and were proof that when the community bands together, our force is so much mightier than we have been taught.

❧ ❧ ❧ ❧

When Robert Martin aka Stephen Donaldson aka Donny the Punk (1946-1996) entered his second year at Columbia University in 1966, he did so as an openly bisexual cisman who was ready to organize and build a community. After being inspired by the

Mattachine Society and his lover, activist Frank Kameny (1925-2011), Donaldson decided to form a queer organization of his own, one that was meant for the students of Columbia. During his Fall semester, he partnered with fellow gay student, James Millham, to start the Student Homophile League (SHL), which still operates, now named the Columbia Queer Alliance. The SHL was slow going, since Columbia required a member list in order to be recognized, and no one except the two founders wanted their names to be public record. Donaldson was a strategist, however, and began to enlist popular, high-ranking students to join as ally members, growing membership and allowing the SHL to be officially recognized in April 1967, making it the first documented LGBTQIA+ college organization. Though he had promised the school that the group would make little noise, Donaldson very much crossed his fingers when he said that, because he immediately began his campaign of queer education and advocacy. He spoke on the school's radio station, interviewed with the school paper, and sent letters to major news outlets, and finally caught the attention of a *New York Times* journalist. An article ran on the front page of the May 3, 1967, issue of the *NYT* that quoted Donaldson on the SHL mission, "we wanted to get the academic community to support equal rights for homosexuals." The article led to a surge in membership, and the founding of chapters at other universities around the country. Donaldson continued his activism work through college but ended up moving away from the homophile movement when he graduated in 1970, due to biphobia. Donaldson's long-term partner was a ciswoman, and this created friction among the gay cismen with whom he worked. Not one to let adversity stand in his way, Donaldson joined the Navy, where after serving two years, he was given a general discharge for being queer, which he fought for years to upgrade to honorable (it was in 1977), and he began his work in bisexual activism. He spoke publicly about bisexuality from a cismale perspective in a way that had yet to be, discussing the notion that bisexuality is "more threatening" than gay or lesbian identities, in the fact that it (like gender non-conforming people with the gender binary) "undermines" the belief in the binary of sexuality. Besides speaking and writing, Donaldson was involved in protests over several different political issues, one of these protests in Washington DC leading to his arrest. **Trigger warning, discussion of rape and assault** While in jail awaiting his bail hearing, a fellow prisoner attacked and raped Donaldson, and this mentally and physically traumatic event led to his requiring not only counseling, but also surgery. He began to suffer from panic attacks, depression, and PTSD, but he was able to muster the strength to use his trauma for activism. Donaldson held a press conference where he vulnerably discussed his attack and became the first male survivor of prison rape to publicly detail their ordeal. Prison reform, particularly in relation to sexual assaults, would become yet another layer of Donaldson's activism, and a core part of Donny the Punk's identity. He would continue to be an active subculture member until he passed away due to complications from AIDS, but his status as a legend in the community continues.

ༀ ༀ ༀ ༀ

The life and medical abuse of David Reimer (1965-2004) may not be, on the surface, part of queer history, but it absolutely fuels support for the fight for intersex and transgender equality and understanding. **Trigger warning on medical abuse** Reimer and his brother were born two perfectly healthy, cismale twins in Manitoba, Canada in August 1965, but by March of the following year their mother noticed the boys were having trouble urinating, so on medical advice, she brought her seven-month-old twins in to be circumcised. The hospital took Reimer (then named Bruce) in to be operated on first, but the surgery went horrendously wrong, and his penis was burned beyond repair, so his brother's surgery was immediately cancelled, and it turned out he did not need the surgery, and the urinary issue cleared on its own. Psychologist and sexologist, John Money (1921-2007), who believed that gender identity was completely nurture-based and none of it was nature, advised Reimer's parents to raise him as female because he was presumed to be not sexually functioning as a male, which apparently was the only determining factor in identity. At twenty-two months old, Reimer underwent surgery to remove his testes and form the external female-assigned sex characteristics. The inappropriate medical interventions did not stop there: Money had the twins in therapy, if you can call it that, where they were made to simulate heterosexual sex acts with each other, as a means to "teach" gender roles to Reimer. After extreme bouts of depression, and suicidal thoughts, Reimer's parents finally told him about his origins, and at fourteen, he began to live the life he always wanted to live, as a man. He lived a relatively quiet life, marrying a woman in 1990, and doing handyman jobs here and there. Then in 1997, he was approached about his story and going public, to discourage future medical professionals from doing this to another human, and Reimer agreed. His story was featured in newspapers and TV programs around the world, it was made into a book, and a *Rolling Stone* article that won a National Magazine Award. Reimer was not able to adequately handle all the attention combined with the depression he had dealt with his entire life. After marital difficulties and the loss of his brother, Reimer ended up passing away due to suicide at thirty-eight. Reimer, just like any transgender or intersex, or even cis, human, was simply who he was; he was born that way. He could not be made into something he was not, no matter how hard the medical community tried to will it. The horrific experience that he went through speaks so deeply to the fight to end intersex surgeries on infants, and to the understanding that transgender and gender non-conforming people are just simply that, transgender and gender non-conforming. Though society may impose boundaries on what characteristics we assign to what genders, those labels do not change the core of what defines each individual's identity.

❧ ❧ ❧ ❧

"I go up to this queen and I say, 'What's your name?' The queen says, 'Monique.' And you say, 'That's marvelous, darling, but what was your name before?' And the queen will look at you straight in the eye and say, 'There was no before.'" Those iconic lines were

spoken by Flawless Sabrina (Jack Doroshow, 1939-2017) at the beginning of the legendary drag documentary, *The Queen* (1968). *The Queen* and its lesser known twenty-two-minute counterpart, *Queen at Heart* (c.1965), were documentaries that honestly covered the experiences of gay men and transwomen who perform as drag queens, and their daily lives dealing with everything from family issues to the draft. *Queen at Heart*, which was filmed as an interview/panel, specifically delved into the lives of transwomen, who were also drag queens. The interviewer asked questions about hormone therapy, dating, and what it is to transition in a world that literally says it is illegal to be you. Though most of the questions would absolutely be considered transphobic now, the ending point and overall intent was to show that no one should judge how another lives their life. *The Queen*, in a more traditional documentary form, follows the contestants and pageant director of the 1967 Nationals: Miss All-America Camp Beauty Pageant. Doroshow, the twenty-four-year-old director and pageant emcee, was self-described as a 110-year-old bar mitzvah mother in drag, and he found joy in creating one of the most prominent drag pageant networks of the time, so prominent that Andy Warhol (1928-1987) was a judge for the 1967 event. The documentary follows the queens as they prepare for the pageants, documenting everything in detail from dance rehearsals to the secret tips and tricks of creating the most perfect cleavage crease, and beyond that it shares a personal look into the daily lives of the gay men and transwomen behind the queens. In intimate interviews in the hotel rooms, the contestants share what relationships are like, how family dynamics work, and how even when they want to serve in the military, they are removed from the draft. As one queen shares, he even wrote to the president, asking to serve in the army, to which he received a letter back that stated it was an honorable desire, and they could not have him in the army now but, "maybe one day we will. We'll see." Each contestant has a unique, and yet familiar, story but the two standouts of the show are eventual winner, Rachel Harlow (b. 1948) and fourth place queen (but the real star), Crystal LaBeija (d.1993). LaBeija, who founded the drag House of LaBeija, throws the most quintessential queen tantrum due to the results of the pageant, which as a viewer is pretty valid. Her five-minute rant about the tomfoolery of the pageant is one of the most iconic and quotable moments in queer herstory. Harlow, the clear favorite from the moment she appears on screen, is quiet, considered naturally beautiful, and is the effective drag daughter of Flawless Sabrina. Her win of the 1967 Nationals was just the beginning of her story, however, as the screening of the film at the Cannes Film Festival sent her to mild fame. She was able to start her social and medical transition, book a few minor roles in film, and even dated John B. Kelly Jr. (1927-1985), the four-time Olympian, brother of screen queen Grace Kelly, and an all-American heartthrob. Harlow was and is an icon of trans experience who has inspired countless queer generations with her story: one famous person who noted her as an inspiration was androgynous legend, David Bowie (1947-2016).

"It really should have been called the Stonewall Uprising. They really were objecting to how they were being treated. That's more an uprising than a riot." These words were spoken by Howard Smith, a reporter for the *Village Voice*, who was inside the Stonewall Inn during the early morning hours of June 28, 1969, and they could not be more true. Stonewall was not the beginning of the gay rights movement, but it was a catalyst that showed the police, government, and cis/het society as a whole, that the LGBTQIA+ community is vast, strong, and would no longer go quietly into obscurity. The Stonewall Inn, which was part of a network of unlicensed bars run by the mafia in New York, catered exclusively to the queer community. In 1969, being gay and/or dressing in clothing that did not match your sex assigned at birth was illegal in forty-nine of fifty states, so underground bars were the communities' only option. The mafia, ever the capitalists, created the bars knowing this fact and though they were known to be seedy, and to water down their drinks, these spaces were home to the thriving queer community, nonetheless. The mafia had deals with the police departments in order to keep the places running and would pay off the cops to only raid during slower hours at the bars. These arrangements worked for periods of time, but with the "clean up the streets" mentality of Mayor John Lindsay (which also reared its head during the 1964 World's Fair in NY), the moral offense department of the NYPD was in full force. The police had already raided Stonewall on

Tuesday, June 24, so the staff and the patrons were shocked when at 1:20am on June 28 the lights flicked on and a voice yelled out, "Police. We are taking the place." There were six police officers and approximately 205 patrons inside, and on this night, the queer people recognized their numbers. The cops began checking gender markers on IDs to the clothing people were wearing and started arresting patrons. As they started taking a masculine presenting lesbian named Stormé DeLarverie (1920-2014) out in handcuffs, she began to push back, yelling that the cuffs were too tight. The police reacted by beating her, which enraged the crowd that was forming outside. They began chanting "pig" and throwing whatever they could at the officers, with a legend of Marsha "Pay it no mind" Johnson (1945-1992), the vocal, badass, Black, transfeminine, sex worker activist, throwing the first brick to ignite the revolution. When the 6th precinct paddy wagon came and went, the original six officers were again alone, but this time with a crowd of well over 500 people. The years of anger, rejection, beatings, arrests, castrations, institutionalizations, and general oppression had boiled to a head that night, and the crowd pushed forward, causing the six officers to barricade themselves inside of Stonewall. By 5am, the tactical police reinforcements had arrived in buses, but the queer community was ready to fight, and dance. Drag queens both used a parking meter as a battering ram and did a kick line where they sang showtunes. Every time the cops tried to corner the crowd, the crowd turned around and cornered the police. The night ended in makeshift Molotov cocktails being thrown, windows shattered, arrests made, queer people beaten, but also a revolution started. The next day a local queer bookstore printed 5,000 leaflets calling attention to the raid and attacks, as well as calling out the corrupt relationship between the mafia and police department. In defiance of the police, Stonewall boarded up its broken windows, replaced the jukebox, and opened for June 28th's evening crowd, and the uprising and raids continued, even larger than the previous night. Hundreds of people came out for six nights in a row, queer people and allies alike. As John O'Brien said in the documentary, *Stonewall Uprising*, "in the peace movement, we ran from the police. That night, the police ran from us, the lowliest of the low. It was fantastic." It was in these nights of actually fighting back that the homophile movement effectively died, the idea of assimilation, of erasing pieces of oneself to be accepted was no longer the goal of the LGBTQIA+ community, because the community realized that they had the power to make change already. Within six months of the uprising, multiple new activist groups were formed, like the Gay Liberation Front and the Gay Activists Alliance, which took aim at making large scale change for queer equity. The first Pride marches came out of these new activist groups, as well. The community did not want the memory of those six days at Stonewall to fade into obscurity like so much of queer history, so they decided to host a march on June 28, 1970. The march started with about 120 people down by Stonewall, and by the time they made it to Central Park the march had thousands of participants and stretched over fifteen blocks. The Stonewall Uprising gave an outlet for the rage and pain that so many in the community were feeling, and then it also gave them a sense of belonging and family that so many lacked; it showed a community that was (is) constantly told they are weak and less than, that they have just been lied to, and there has always been great power in being queer.

Bibliography

Belonsky, Andrew. "New York's First Ever Anti-Gay Raid At The Ariston Baths (February 21, 1903)." *Towle Road*, 8 Oct. 2010, www.towleroad.com/2010/10/remembering-the-ariston-baths-new-yorks-first-anti-gay-raid/.

Marino, Henrique. "Pedro and Muño, The First Gay Wedding in Spain ... in the Year 1061." *Publico*, 18 Nov. 2020, www.publico.es/sociedad/primera-boda-gay-matrimonio-homosexual.html.

"(1963) Josephine Baker, 'Speech at the March on Washington' •." Translated by BlackPast, *Black Past*, 23 Sept. 2019, www.blackpast.org/african-american-history/speeches-african-american-history/1963-josephine-baker-speech-march-washington/.

Aldrich, Robert, and Garry Wotherspoon. *Who's Who in Gay and Lesbian History*. Routledge, 2002.

Alexeyeff, Kalissa. *Dancing from the Heart: Movement, Gender, and Cook Islands Globalization*. University of Hawai'i Press, 2009.

Amer, Sahar. *Crossing Borders: Love Between Women in Medieval French and Arabic Literatures*. University of Pennsylvania Press, 2008.

Asprey, Robert B. *Frederick the Great: The Magnificent Enigma*. Neb., 2007.

Badcock, James. "The Lesbian Pioneers Who Fooled Spain's Catholic Church." *BBC News*, 19 Feb. 2018, www.bbc.com/news/world-europe-43057841.

Baker, Paul. *Fantabulosa: a Dictionary of Polari and Gay Slang*. Continuum, 2004.

Bartlett, Nancy H., and Paul L. Vasey. "A Retrospective Study of Childhood Gender-Atypical Behavior in Samoan Fa'Afafine." *Archives of Sexual Behavior*, vol. 35, no. 6, 2006, pp. 659–666., doi:10.1007/s10508-006-9055-1.

Bauer, Thomas. "Male-Male Love in Classical Arabic Poetry." *The Cambridge History of Gay and Lesbian Literature*, by McCallum and Tuhkanen, Cambridge University Press, 2014, pp. 107–124.

Beaumont, Charles. "The Crooked Man." *Playboy*, June 2017, www.playboy.com/read/the-crooked-man.

Blanchard, Mary W. "The Soldier and the Aesthete: Homosexuality and Popular Culture in Gilded Age America." *Journal of American Studies*, vol. 30, no. 1, 1996, pp. 25–46., doi: 10.1017/s0021875800024300.

"Bob Mizer." *Bob Mizer Foundation*, 2017, www.bobmizer.org/bobmizer.

Borgos, Anna. "Sándor/Sarolta Vay, a Gender Bender in Fin-De-Siècle Hungary." *Comparative Hungarian Cultural Studies*, 2011, pp. 220–231., doi:10.2307/j.ctt6wq7fz.20.

Borris, Kenneth. *Same-Sex Desire in the English Renaissance: A Sourcebook of Texts, 1470-1650*. Routledge, 2015.

Boyd, Nan Alamilla. *Wide-Open Town: a History of Queer San Francisco to 1965*. University of California Press, 2003.

Briker, Gregory. "The Right to Be Heard: ONE Magazine, Obscenity Law, and the Battle Over Homosexual Speech." *Yale Journal of Law & Humanities*, vol. 31, no. 1, 2020, pp. 49–74.

Brooten, Bernadette J. *Love between Women: Early Christian Responses to Female Homoeroticism*. University of Chicago Press, 1998.

Brown, Kathleen M. "'Changed ... into the Fashion of Man' The Politics of Sexual Difference in a Seventeenth-Century Anglo-American Settlement." *Journal of the History of Sexuality*, vol. 6, no. 2, Oct. 1995, pp. 171–193., doi:10.1093/acprof:oso/9780195112436.003.0004.

Bullough, Vern L. "Alfred Kinsey and the Kinsey Report: Historical Overview and Lasting Contributions." *Journal of Sex Research*, vol. 35, no. 2, 1998, pp. 127–131., doi: 10.1080/00224499809551925.

Burroway, Jim. "An Innocent Man: The Surprising Trial of Dale Jennings." *Emphasis Mine*, 9 Aug. 2018, jimburroway.com/history/an-innocent-man-the-surprising-trial-of-dale-jennings/.

Caisou-Rousseau, Inger Littberger. *Therese Andreas Bruce: En sällsam Historia Fraan 1800-Talet: levnadsberättelse, Brev Och Verser Med Inledning Och Kommentarer*. Makadam, 2013.

Capers, I. Bennet. "Cross Dressing and the Criminal." *Yale Journal of Law and the*

Humanities, vol. 20, 2008, pp. 1–30.

Carter, Jacoby Adeshei. "Alain LeRoy Locke." *Stanford Encyclopedia of Philosophy*, Stanford University, 23 Mar. 2012, plato.stanford.edu/entries/alain-locke/.

Chandler, Glenn. *Sins of Jack Saul: The True Story of Dublin Jack and the Cleveland Street Scandal.* Grosvenor House Publishing Ltd, 2016.

Chauncey, George. *Gay New York: Gender, Urban Culture, and the Making of the Gay Male World, 1890-1940.* Basic Books, 2019.

Chotzner, J. "Kalonymos Ben Kalonymos, a Thirteenth-Century Satirist." *The Jewish Quarterly Review*, vol. 13, no. 1, 1900, p. 128., doi:10.2307/1450670.

Clark, Anna. "Anne Lister's Construction of Lesbian Identity." *Journal of the History of Sexuality*, vol. 7, no. 1, July 1996, pp. 23–50., doi:www.jstor.org/stable/3840441.

Clarke, John. *Roman Sex: 100 BC to AD 250.* ECHO POINT Books & MEDIA, 2014.

Cleves, Rachel Hope. *Charity and Sylvia: A Same-Sex Marriage in Early America.* Oxford University Press, 2017.

Colapinto, John. "The True Story of John/Joan." *Rolling Stone*, Dec. 1997, pp. 54–97.

Crompton, Louis. *Homosexuality & Civilization.* Belknap Press, 2006.

Cromwell, Jason. *Transmen and FTMs: Identities, Bodies, Genders, and Sexualities.* University of Illinois Press, 1999.

Cunnington, Phillis, and Catherine Lucas. *Costume for Births, Marriages and Deaths.* Black, 1978.

Cutpurse, Moll, and Randall S. Nakayama. *The Life and Death of Mrs. Mary Frith: Commonly Called Moll Cutpurse, 1662 with a Facsimile of the Original Edition.* Garland, 1993.

Davis, Kate and David Heilbroner, directors. *Stonewall Uprising.* PBS, 2010.

de la Cretaz, Britni. "The Hidden Queer History Behind 'A League of Their Own.'" *Narratively*, 19 Mar. 2021, narratively.com/the-hidden-queer-history-behind-a-league-of-their-own/.

Dempsey, Hugh A. *The Vengeful Wife and Other Blackfoot Stories.* University Of Oklahoma Press, 2006.

DeVun, Leah. "Heavenly Hermaphrodites: Sexual Difference at the Beginning and End of Time." *Postmedieval*, vol. 9, no. 2, 2018, pp. 132–146., doi:10.1057/s41280-018-0080-8.

Diaz, Robert. "The Limits OfBaklaand Gay: Feminist Readings OfMy Husband's Lover, Vice Ganda, and Charice Pempengco." *Signs: Journal of Women in Culture and Society*, vol. 40, no. 3, 2015, pp. 721–745., doi: 10.1086/679526.

Doniger, Wendy. "The 'Kamasutra': It Isn't All about Sex." *The Kenyon Review*, vol. 25, no. 1, 2003, pp. 18–37., www.jstor.org/stable/4338414.

Donovan, Brian. *Respectability on Trial: Sex Crimes in New York City, 1900-1918.* State University of New York Press, 2016.

Dose, Ralf, and Edward H. Willis. *Magnus Hirschfeld: and the Origins of the Gay Liberation Movement.* Monthly Review Press, 2014.

Du Preez, Michael, and Jeremy Dronfield. *Dr James Barry: A Woman Ahead of Her Time.* Oneworld, 2017.

Duggan, Elizabeth A. "Hall, Murray H." *Encyclopedia.com*, Encyclopedia of Lesbian, Gay, Bisexual and Transgender History in America, 2019, www.encyclopedia.com/social-sciences/encyclopedias-almanacs-transcripts-and-maps/hall-murray-h.

Dynes, Wayne R. *Encyclopedia of Homosexuality.* Routledge, 2017.

Eisenbichler, Konrad. *The Sword and the Pen: Women, Politics, and Poetry in Sixteenth-Century Siena.* University of Notre Dame Press, 2012.

Ellis, Albert. "Constitutional Factors in Homosexuality: A Re-Examination of the Evidence." *Advances in Sex Research*, vol. 1, Oct. 1963, pp. 161–186., doi:https://www.jstor.org/stable/3811210?acceptTC=true&seq=1.

Espinoza, Lucas E., and Rosalva Resendiz. "Los Secretos De La Redada De Los 41 (The Secrets of the Raid of the 41): A Sociohistorical Analysis of a Gay Signifier." *NACCS Annual Conference Proceedings*, 1 Apr. 2018, scholarworks.sjsu.edu/cgi/viewcontent.cgi?article=1197&context=naccs.

Estrada, Gabriel. "Two Spirits, Nádleeh, and LGBTQ2 Navajo Gaze." *American Indian*

Culture and Research Journal, vol. 35, no. 4, 2011, pp. 167–190., doi:10.17953/aicr.35.4.x500172017344j30.

"Eve Addams' Ring of Rich Cultists." *Variety Magazine*, 28 July 1926, p. 37.

Faderman, Lillian, and Stuart Timmons. *Gay L.A.: A History of Sexual Outlaws, Power Politics, and Lipstick Lesbians*. University of California Press, 2009.

Faderman, Lillian. *To Believe in Women: What Lesbians Have Done For America - A History*. Houghton Mifflin, 2000.

Farquhar, Michael. *A Treasury of Royal Scandals: The Shocking True Stories of History's Wickedest, Weirdest, Most Wanton Kings, Queens, Tsars, Popes, and Emperors*. Penguin Books, 2001.

Fleming, E. J. *The Fixers: Eddie Mannix, Howard Strickling, and the MGM Publicity Machine*. McFarland & Co., 2005.

Funke, Jana. "The Case of Karl M.[Artha] Baer: Narrating 'Uncertain' Sex." *Sex, Gender and Time in Fiction and Culture*, 2011, pp. 132–153., doi:10.1057/9780230307087_8.

Gallo, M. M. "Different Daughters." *OAH Magazine of History*, vol. 20, no. 2, 2006, pp. 27–30., doi:10.1093/maghis/20.2.27.

Gesink, Indira Falk. "Intersex Bodies in Premodern Islamic Discourse." *Journal of Middle East Women's Studies*, vol. 14, no. 2, 2018, pp. 152–173., doi: 10.1215/15525864-6680205.

Gever, Martha. *Entertaining Lesbians: Celebrity, Sexuality, and Self-Invention*. Routledge, 2003.

Goldberg, Jeremy. " John Rykener, Richard II, and the Governance of London." *Leeds Studies in English*, ser. 45, 31 Dec. 2014, pp. 49–70. *45*.

Graham, Sharyn. "Sex, Gender, and Priests in South Sulawesi, Indonesia." *International Institute for Asian Studies Newletter*, Nov. 2002, p. 27.

Hermary, Antoine. "Building Power: Palaces and the Built Environment in Cyprus in the Archaic and Classical Periods." *Bulletin of the American Schools of Oriental Research*, vol. 370, 2013, pp. 83–101., doi:10.5615/bullamerschoorie.370.0083.

Higgs, David. *Queer Sites: Gay Urban Histories Since 1600*. Routledge, 2003.

Hill, Abram. "The Hamilton Lodge Ball." *Schomburg Center for Research in Black Culture, Manuscripts, Archives and Rare Books Division*, New York Public Library, 1939, digitalcollections.nypl.org/items/16910cf0-7cf4-0133-46b1-00505686d14e#/?uuid=16acce70-7cf4-0133-d749-00505686d14e.

Holland, Merlin. *The Real Trial of Oscar Wilde*. Harper Collins, 2004.

Holloway, Robert. *The Phoenix of Sodom; Or, the Vere Street Coterie, Etc*. J. Cook, 1813.

Horswell, Michael J. *Decolonizing the Sodomite: Queer Tropes of Sexuality in Colonial Andean Culture*. University of Texas Press, 2006.

Huang, Hans Tao-Ming. *Queer Politics and Sexual Modernity in Taiwan*. Hong Kong University Press, 2011.

Hubbard, T.K. "Popular Perceptions of Elite Homosexuality in Classical Athens." *Arion: A Journal of Humanities and the Classics*, vol. 6, no. 1, ser. 3, 1998, pp. 48–78. *JSTOR*, www.jstor.org/stable/20163707.

Iglikowski-Broad, Vicky. "'Lady Austin's Camp Boys'." *The National Archives* , United Kingdom Government, 5 Feb. 2015, blog.nationalarchives.gov.uk/lady-austins-camp-boys/.

JACKSON, JEFFREY H. *PAPER BULLETS: Two Artists Who Risked Their Lives to Defy the Nazis*. ALGONQUIN OF CHAPEL HILL, 2020.

Joseph, Channing Gerard. "The First Drag Queen Was a Former Slave." *The Nation*, 31 Jan. 2020, www.thenation.com/article/society/drag-queen-slave-ball/.

Kamiya, Gary. "Drag Act Turned Black Cat Cafe into Gay Bar in 2nd Life." *SFGATE*, San Francisco Chronicle, 8 Nov. 2014, www.sfgate.com/bayarea/article/Drag-act-turned-Black-Cat-Cafe-into-gay-bar-in-5879015.php.

Kates, Gary. "The Transgendered World of the Chevalier/Chevalière D'Eon." *The Journal of Modern History*, vol. 67, no. 3, 1995, pp. 558–594., doi:10.1086/245173.

Katz, Jonathan Ned. *Love Stories: Sex Between Men Before Homosexuality*. University of Chicago Press, 2013.

Keats, John. *You Might As Well Live: The Life and Times of Dorothy Parker*. Secker &

Warburg, 1970.

Kilaru, Rakesh N., and Chanakya A. Sethi. "Brief of Historians as Amici Curiae In Support of Employees." *Supreme Court of the United States Dockets*, July 2019, www.supremecourt.gov/DocketPDF/18/18-107/107152/20190703162401867_Title%20VII%20Historians%20Brief%20PDFA.pdf.

Kistler, Alan. "How the 'Code Authority' Kept LGBT Characters Out of Comics." *History.com*, A&E Television Networks, 28 Apr. 2017, www.history.com/news/how-the-code-authority-kept-lgbt-characters-out-of-comics.

Larson, Scott. "'Indescribable Being': Theological Performances of Genderlessness in the Society of the Publick Universal Friend, 1776–1819." *Early American Studies: An Interdisciplinary Journal*, vol. 12, no. 3, 2014, pp. 576–600. *Beyond the Binaries: Critical Approaches to Sex and Gender in Early America*, doi:10.1353/eam.2014.0020.

Lavelle, Brian M. *The Sorrow and the Pity: a Prolegomenon to a History of Athens Under the Peisistratids, c. 560-510 B.C.* Steiner, 1993.

"LAY NAVY SCANDAL TO F.D. ROOSEVELT." *New York Times*, 21 July 1921, p. 4, timesmachine.nytimes.com/timesmachine/1921/07/20/109814482.html?pageNumber=4.

Lehrman, Sally. "Billy Tipton: Self-Made Man." *Stanford Today Online*, 1997, web.stanford.edu/dept/news/stanfordtoday/ed/9705/9705fea601.shtml.

Linderman, Frank Bird. *Pretty-Shield: Medicine Woman of the Crows*. Univ. of Nebraska Press, 2003.

Lipsky, W. *Gay and Lesbian San Francisco*. Arcadia, 2006.

Lyon, William S. *Encyclopedia of Native American Healing*. NetLibrary, Inc., 1999.

Madsen, Axel. *The Sewing Circle: Hollywood's Greatest Secret-- Female Stars Who Loved Other Women*. Open Road Media, 2015.

Manalo-Camp, Adam Keawe. "Māhū Resistance: Challenging Colonial Structures of Power and Gender." *Medium.com*, 8 Aug. 2020, medium.com/@adamkeawe/m%C4%81h%C5%AB-resistance-challenging-colonial-structures-of-power-and-gender-6f0c1e96cded.

McKenna, Neil. *The Secret Life of Oscar Wilde*. Basic Books, 2006.

Medicine, Beatrice. "Directions in Gender Research in American Indian Societies: Two Spirits and Other Categories." *Online Readings in Psychology and Culture*, vol. 3, no. 1, 2002, doi:10.9707/2307-0919.1024.

Mehra, Bharat, et al. "An Exploratory Journey of Cultural Visual Literacy of 'Non-Conforming' Gender Representations from Pre-Colonial Sub- Saharan Africa." *Open Information Science*, vol. 3, no. 1, 2019, pp. 1–21., doi:10.1515/opis-2019-0001.

Milar, Katharine S. "The Myth Buster." *Monitor on Psychology*, American Psychological Association, Feb. 2011, www.apa.org/monitor/2011/02/myth-buster.

Mina, Maria. "Anthropomorphic Figurines from the Neolithic and Early Bronze Age Aegean: Gender Dynamics and Implications for the Understanding of Aegean Prehistory." University of London, 2006.

Minter, Shannon. "Sodomy and Public Morality Offenses under U.S. Immigration Law: Penalizing Lesbian and Gay Identity." *Cornell International Law Journal*, vol. 26, no. 3, 1993, pp. Article 11.

Mondello, Bob. "Remembering Hollywood's Hays Code, 40 Years On." *NPR*, NPR, 8 Aug. 2008, www.npr.org/templates/story/story.php?storyId=93301189.

Morgan, Ruth, and Graeme Reid. "'I've Got Two Men and One Woman': Ancestors, Sexuality and Identity among Same-Sex Identified Women Traditional Healers in South Africa." *Culture, Health & Sexuality*, vol. 5, no. 5, 2003, pp. 375–391., doi: 10.1080/1369105011000064146.

Morgan, Thad. "When Hollywood Studios Married Off Gay Stars to Keep Their Sexuality a Secret." *History.com*, A&E Television Networks, 10 July 2019, www.history.com/news/hollywood-lmarriages-gay-stars-lgbt.

Morrison, Amani C., and Tracy Heather Strain. "Looking for Lorraine: The Radiant and Radical Life of Lorraine Hansberry ." *African American Review*, vol. 53, no. 3, 2020, pp. 251–254., doi:10.1353/afa.2020.0038.

Moske, Jim. "Stephen Donaldson Papers, 1965-1996." *The New York Public Library Humanities and Social Sciences Library Manuscripts and Archives Division*, Sept. 2000, web.archive.org/web/20080512013008/www.nypl.org/research/chss/spe/rbk/faids/donaldson.pdf.

Murray, Stephen O. *Pacific Homosexualities.* Writers Club Press, 2002.

Murray, Stephen O., et al. *Islamic Homosexualities: Culture, History, and Literature.* New York University Press, 1997.

Nelson, William E. "Criminality and Sexual Morality in New York, 1920-1980." *Yale Journal of Law & the Humanities*, vol. 5, no. 2, 1993, pp. 265–341.

Nestle, Joan. "Excerpts from the Oral History of Mabel Hampton." *Signs: Journal of Women in Culture and Society*, vol. 18, no. 4, 1993, pp. 925–935., doi:10.1086/494849.

Newton, David E. *Gay and Lesbian Rights: A Reference Handbook.* ABC-CLIO, 2009.

Norton, Rictor. *My Dear Boy: Gay Love Letters through the Centuries.* Leyland Publications, 1998.

"The Origins of the Cake Walk." *The Journal of Blacks in Higher Education*, no. 35, 2002, p. 134., doi:10.2307/3133884.

Ovid, et al. *Metamorphoses.* W. W. Norton & Company, 2021.

Pak Si-Baek uĭ Chosŏn Wangjo Sillok = *The Annals of the Joseon Dynasty*, by Si-baek Pak, Humanist, 2015, pp. vol. 46-vol. 75.

Pear, Robert. "Ban Is Affirmed on Homosexuals Entering the Nation." *The New York Times*, 27 Dec. 1979, p. 16.

Peralta, Eyder. "Researchers Dig Up 'Homosexual Or Transsexual' Caveman Near Prague." *NPR*, 11 Apr. 2011, www.npr.org/sections/thetwo-way/2011/04/08/135212785/researchers-dig-up-homosexual-or-transsexual-caveman-near-prague.

Prigge, Matthew J. "The 'Girl-Man' of Milwaukee: The Lives of Cora Anderson." *The Wisconsin Magazine of History*, vol. 96, no. 3, 2013, pp. 14–27. *JSTOR*, www.jstor.org/stable/24401945.

Reeder, Greg. "Same-Sex Desire, Conjugal Constructs, and the Tomb of Niankhkhnum and Khnumhotep." *World Archaeology*, vol. 32, no. 2, 2000, pp. 193–208., doi: 10.1080/00438240050131180.

Robertson, JD. "Lesbian Icon Ruth Ellis." *The Velvet Chronicle*, 29 Sept. 2020, thevelvetchronicle.com/lesbian-icon-ruth-ellis/.

Roscoe, Will, et al. *Boy-Wives and Female Husbands: Studies in African Homosexualities.* Palgrave, 1998.

Rowbotham, Judith. "A Deception on the Public: The Real Scandal of Boulton and Park." *Liverpool Law Review*, vol. 36, no. 2, 2015, pp. 123–145., doi:10.1007/s10991-015-9158-7.

Rowson, Everett K. "The Effeminates of Early Medina." *Journal of the American Oriental Society*, vol. 111, no. 4, 1991, p. 671., doi: 10.2307/603399.

Rupp, Leila J. "Transnational Homophile Organizing: The International Committee for Sexual Equality." American Historical Association, *125th Annual Meeting American Historical Association*, 2011, www.researchgate.net/publication/267535851_Transnational_Homophile_Organizing_The_International_Committee_for_Sexual_Equality.

Sappho, et al. *Sappho: a New Translation of the Complete Works.* Cambridge University Press, 2015.

Scagliotti, John, director. *Before Homosexuals.* The Center for Independent Documentary, 2017.

Schiff , Judith Ann. "Dual-Career Couple." *Old Yale*, Yale Alumni Magazine, 2014, yalealumnimagazine.com/articles/3912-dual-career-couple.

Sears, Clare. *"A Dress Not Belonging to His or Her Sex: Cross-Dressing Law in San Francisco, 1860-1900.* University of California, Santa Cruz, 2005.

"The Sex Changes That Made History." Hayes-Fisher, John, director. Season 1, episode 1, BBC, 2015.

Shaheen, Aaron. "Strolling through the Slums of the Past: Ralph Werther's Love Affair with Victorian Womanhood in 'Autobiography of an Androgyne.'" *PMLA/Publications of the Modern Language Association of America*, vol. 128, no. 4, 2013, pp. 923–937., doi:10.1632/pmla.2013.128.4.923.

Shilts, Randy. *Conduct Unbecoming: Gays and Lesbians in the U.S. Military.* St. Martin's Griffin, 2005.

Sibilla, Nick. "How Liquor Licenses Sparked the Stonewall Riots." *Reason.com*, Reason, 28 June 2015, reason.com/2015/06/28/how-liquor-licenses-sparked-stonewall/.

Simon, Frank, director. *The Queen*. Si Litvinoff Vineyard Films-MDH Enterprises Production, 1968.

Smith, A. "QUEER THEORY AND NATIVE STUDIES: The Heteronormativity of Settler Colonialism." *GLQ: A Journal of Lesbian and Gay Studies*, vol. 16, no. 1-2, 2010, pp. 41–68., doi:10.1215/10642684-2009-012.

Somerset, Anne. *The Affair of the Poisons: Murder, Infanticide, and Satanism at the Court of Louis XIV*. Phoenix, 2004.

Soyer, Francois. *Ambiguous Gender in Early Modern Spain and Portugal: Inquisitors, Doctors and the Transgression of Gender Norms*. Brill, 2012.

Stein, Marc. *Rethinking the Gay and Lesbian Movement*. Taylor & Francis Ltd, 2012.

Stern, Keith, and Ian McKellen. *Queers in History: the Comprehensive Encyclopedia of Historical Gays, Lesbians, Bisexuals, and Transgenders*. BenBella Books, Inc., 2009.

Stevenson, Matilda Coxe. *The Zuni Indians: Their Mythology, Esoteric Fraternities, and Ceremonies*. Nabu Press, 2010.

Strong, Lester Q. "Josephine Baker's Hungry Heart." *The Gay & Lesbian Review*, 6 Feb. 2020, glreview.org/article/article-959/.

Suzuki, Michiko. "Writing Same-Sex Love: Sexology and Literary Representation in Yoshiya Nobuko's Early Fiction." *The Journal of Asian Studies*, vol. 65, no. 3, 2006, pp. 575–599., doi:10.1017/s0021911806001148.

***Symposium*,** by Plato and Johann Gottfried Stallbaum, Garland, 1980.

Treuer, Anton. *The Assassination of Hole in the Day*. Borealis Books, 2011.

"The Trial of Mother Clap for Keeping a Sodomitical House." *Secret Sexualities*, 2003, pp. 82–82., doi:10.4324/9780203360316-9.

Tulchin, Allan A. "Same-Sex Couples Creating Households in Old Regime France: The Uses of the Affrèrement." *The Journal of Modern History*, vol. 79, no. 3, 2007, pp. 613–647., doi: 10.1086/517983.

Turley, Hans. *Rum, Sodomy, and the Lash: Piracy, Sexuality, and Masculine Identity*. New York University Press, 1999.

United States, Congress, Cong. House. *Homosexuals in Government, 1950*, vol. 96, ser. 4, Congressional Record, 1950, pp. 4527–4528. 81st Congress, 2nd session, document Congressional Record Volume 96, Part 4. *4.*

"Usage Alert About Gay." *Dictionary.com*, 2006, www.dictionary.com/browse/gay.

Varner, Eric R. "Transcending Gender: Assimilation, Identity, and Roman Imperial Portraits." *Memoirs of the American Academy in Rome*, Supplementary Volumes 7, 2008, pp. 185–205., www.jstor.org/stable/40379354.

"Voluptuous Panic: the Erotic World of Weimar Berlin." *Voluptuous Panic the Erotic World of Weimar Berlin*, by Mel Gordon, Feral House, 2008.

Walker, Malaysia. "Highlight: Lucy Hicks Anderson, a Black Trans Pioneer." *ACLU of Mississippi*, 21 Feb. 2018, www.aclu-ms.org/en/news/highlight-lucy-hicks-anderson-black-trans-pioneer.

Watson, Robert P. *Affairs of State: The Untold History of Presidential Love, Sex, and Scandal, 1789–1900*. Rowman & Littlefield Publishers, 2014.

Wei, S. Louisa. "Esther Eng." *Esther Eng – Women Film Pioneers Project*, Columbia University Libraries, 2014, wfpp.columbia.edu/pioneer/esther-eng/.

Whitehouse, Ruth D. "Exploring Gender in Prehistoric Italy." *Papers of the British School at Rome*, vol. 69, 2001, pp. 49–96., doi:10.1017/s0068246200001768.

Wilson, Bianca D. "Black Lesbian Gender and Sexual Culture: Celebration and Resistance." *Culture, Health & Sexuality*, vol. 11, no. 3, Apr. 2009, pp. 297–313., doi: 10.1080/13691050802676876.

Young, Michael B. *King James and the History of Homosexuality*. New York University Press, 2000.

Young, Morgen. "Alan Hart (1890-1962)." *Oregon Encyclopedia*, Oct. 2019, www.oregonencyclopedia.org/articles/hart_alan_1890_1962_/#.YGVW0EXYrrc.

Yuan, Jada, and Aaron Wong. "The First Black Trans Model Had Her Face on a Box of Clairol." *The Cut*, New York Magazine, 15 Dec. 2015, www.thecut.com/2015/12/tracey-africa-transgender-model-c-v-r.html.

www.ingramcontent.com/pod-product-compliance
Lightning Source LLC
LaVergne TN
LVHW052344100826
845147LV00012B/752

* 9 7 8 0 5 7 8 3 2 6 3 8 2 *